Jason Holt

Meanings of Art

Essays in Aesthetics

MINKOWSKI
Institute Press

Jason Holt
School of Kinesiology
Acadia University
550 Main Street
Wolfville, Nova Scotia
Canada B4P 2R6

Cover: A fragment from an abstract drawing by the late Mostafa Showleh, Montreal, Canada

ISBN: 978-1-927763-38-4 (softcover)
ISBN: 978-1-927763-39-1 (ebook)

Minkowski Institute Press
Montreal, Quebec, Canada
http://minkowskiinstitute.org/mip/

For information on all Minkowski Institute Press publications visit our website at http://minkowskiinstitute.org/mip/books/

For Megan, naturally

Preface

This project began over twenty years ago and has continued since sometimes more, sometimes less sporadically. Over the years, owing as much to certain research opportunities as presented themselves as to anything else, it became increasingly clear that this book would not be written fully from scratch but was rather emerging organically and piecemeal in the form of the stand-alone essays collected here. Changes from the original published form of the essays have been minimized, and consist mostly of scant editorial comments and corrections to a fistful of typos and the odd misquotation or error of fact.

The perspective unfolded and defended here is a philosophical theory of art grounded in particular understandings of the creative process, aesthetic experience, and interpretive practice. The thematic link among all of these is the concept of meaning: what it means to make art, how the meanings we attach to artworks in interpretation shape our appreciation, the nature and value of aesthetic experience, and ultimately the definition of art itself. On this view, creating art is an expressive process that, as such, may be left incomplete. Aesthetic experience is understood as a special kind of resolution of conflict between the intellect and the emotions, one resonant with a very old tradition in aesthetics as well as cutting-edge neuroaesthetics. It is because of the deep human need for such experience that this book champions the interpretive openness of artworks and pluralism when it comes to interpretive and critical practice.

Highlights of the book include a blend between more abstract, purely theoretical essays (Part I, "Foundations") and applied essays that do not just illustrate but also by turns illuminate and further build on such theoretical foundations (Part II, "Extensions"). Apart from articulating a unique expressive-aesthetic theory of art together with supporting accounts of artistic creation, interpretation, and appreciation, this book also engages persistent problems in the philosophy of art (e.g., the paradox of fiction, the problem of taste), discusses significant but largely neglected aesthetic aberrations (e.g., "partworks," ex ante allusions), and broaches original definitions and discoveries (e.g., film noir as "stylized crime realism," the foreshadowing in *The Sun Also Rises* of Hemingway's suicide).

Among the many people who merit thanks for contributing in one way or another to this book, I will single out those whose omission would be particularly glaring. First, I thank Steven Burns, who advised me during my first forays into aesthetics as a graduate student. I would also like to thank those colleagues who edited volumes to which some of these essays were originally contributed: William Irwin, Mark T. Conard, Aeon J. Skoble, Steven M. Sanders, Joseph Westfall, Dave Baggett, and William A. Drumin. My close literary friends Astrid Brunner and Liane Heller have been of enormous support over the years. Thanks also go to Vesselin Petkov at the Minkowski Institute Press. Last, to my wife Megan Haliburton, my deepest appreciation.

Contents

Part I

Foundations

1 PARTWORKS

Bach's *The Art of Fugue*, Schubert's *Symphony in B minor*, Mozart's *Requiem*, Michelangelo's *Bearded Slave* and *Atlas*, Rodin's *Gates of Hell*, David's portraiture of Napoleon and Madame Récamier, certain later Cézannes, Flaubert's *Bouvard et Pécuchet*, Kafka's *The Trial* and *The Castle*—all deservedly famous, all provocatively unfinished. As Monroe Beardsley observes, such unfinished works "have a powerful incompleteness—so much so that some people feel compelled to try to complete them.'[1] One thinks of Süssmayr "finishing" the *Requiem*, of Max Brod editing *The Trial* or preserving it in such a form that readers are liable to gloss over the gaps. Unfinished works inspire counterfactual imagining: What would the *Requiem* have sounded like if Mozart had completed it? How might *The Castle* have ended if Kafka had been able to finish it—to his satisfaction? No doubt it is such imagining that inspires efforts to complete the great unfinished works of others, not to mention the obvious cachet of virtue by association.

Setting aside significant moral issues concerning the permissibility of finishing another's work, however artful, however respectful, such "finishings" may be—Mozart and Kafka were in no position to sign off on these works, and indeed Kafka's deathbed request was that Brod have the manuscripts destroyed—cases of unfinished artworks are provocative in other ways as well. Where death interferes with the completion of a great work, the work's posthumous incomplete status serves as a poignant reminder of mortality, a counterpoint to the immortal greatness of the work and the talent that produced it. Aside from such romantic notions, we might be concerned with epistemological issues, the business of identifying unfinished works or determining

---

[1] Monroe C. Beardsley, *Aesthetics: Problems in the Philosophy of Criticism* (Indianapolis: Hackett, 1982), 193.

3

degrees and kinds of incompleteness. Many times one can seemingly tell an unfinished work at a glance, even though, extending Danto's insight, just as indiscernible counterparts may be art and non-art respectively, or completely different artworks with completely different meanings, so too might indiscernibles prove to be finished and unfinished works of art. In many cases there is sufficient contextual information to confirm the perceptual suspicion that a work has not been completed, that the artist has not signed off on it. But although there are often indications, glaring or subtle, that a work is unfinished, it is entirely possible that sometimes we will not be able to tell or will be wrong in particular judgments about the status of certain work as finished or unfinished.

My purpose here is not to explore in any detail these epistemological questions, for we know enough about enough unfinished works to tackle a different, comparably important, and largely neglected set of issues concerning the theoretical status of unfinished artworks, which I somewhat playfully call *partworks*, and the implications they have for fundamental theories of art. I will argue that if we characterize partworks in anything like an intuitive way, according them partial artwork status and neither as full-blown artworks nor as non-artworks *simpliciter*, the implications for art theory will be potentially profound. I will argue that we should accord partworks partial art status, and that current theories of art cannot account or allow for such, as the criteria they provide are not articulated in, and cannot be paraphrased into, a form allowing for a graded conception of the divide between art and non-art that partworks suggest. I will also argue that the kind of graded concept allowing and accounting for partworks and serviceable as an essential supplement to art theory can be found in more traditional approaches to art theory, specifically those that emphasize, over and above simple artefact production, the psychological aspects of the creative process.

1

The first order of business is making clear what exactly I mean by the term 'partworks.' Taking the examples with which I began this paper, partworks are unfinished artworks, unfinished in that more work needs to be done in order to complete them, works on which the artist has typically, and for this reason, not signed off. By signing off on a work, sometimes with an actual signature, sometimes merely with the thought "Yes, that's it," and a moving on to other things, an artist implies at least a minimal satisfaction that the work is in its proper final form (though whether the completed work counts as successful is an entirely different matter). 'Partworks' therefore designates not only works abandoned or left unfinished when artists die, but also works in progress that will, but have yet to be, completed. Throughout the process of Michelangelo sculpting it, *David* was in this sense no less a partwork than *Atlas* has remained to this day. At the moment the work was finished and so deemed by the sculptor himself, the partwork of *David*-in-process became the completed work of sculpture. In the case of lasting partworks, the creative process, once interrupted, has never been resumed.

I would like to further clarify the term 'partworks' by outlining several things that I do not mean by it. For instance, some people are inclined to assert, speaking rather loosely, that all artworks are incomplete, meaning perhaps that every work can be further improved (though this is doubtful in many cases), that all artwork leaves something out (think of the absent Goliath the already massive *David* suggests), that art strictly requires an audience and so in the absence of such is incomplete, or that the history of any artwork is always unfolding, is still being written. Whatever the merits of these views, I mean partworks to refer, in contrast to works which are complete in a more conventional sense, to those that are incomplete in that conventional sense. Nor do partworks include those artworks that exhibit what might be called gappy completeness: orchestral works with cadenzas, fictional narratives with important but aesthetically rewarding omissions, and so on. Also excluded are stand-alone cases, parts of unfinished composite works that count as complete works in themselves, Rodin's *Paolo and Francesca (The Kiss)* vis-à-vis the unfinished *Gates of Hell*, for instance. Sketches and studies in service of future work, as separate from the eventual work itself, should also be excluded, constituting plausible artworks in their own right (as with David's drawing for *Oath of the Tennis Court*) or possibly being relegated to mere non-artistic, though undeniably useful, art auxiliaries (as with some of Magritte's rough sketches and photographs). I also exclude, similarly, artworks that have been envisioned and perhaps prepared for but on which work has not yet begun, as with the fictional paintings in Willeford's *The Burnt Orange Heresy*. A more difficult exclusion, perhaps, is the case of completed but partly destroyed works, such as the *Venus de Milo*. Although there is an obvious sense in which the *Venus* we have is incomplete, missing parts that it used to possess, it should not be counted as partwork. Though constitutively incomplete relative to its uncorrupted predecessor, the *Venus* was, and remains, a finished work. Asymmetries between once-finished and not-yet and never-will-be finished works are too substantial to allow partly destroyed works into the partworks class. In short, partworks do not include any of the following: all art, gappily complete art, stand-alone art, mere preparatory work, merely envisioned art, or partly destroyed art.

The picture of partworks that has been given here is that of a band surrounding the line dividing the artwork class from its non-art complement, of partworks on the road to becoming art, irrespective of whether they ever arrive at the intended destination. This does not mean that partworks are, paradoxically, both art and not art. Strictly put, they are *not* artworks, at least not yet, because more work needs to be done on them and the artist has yet to sign off. A sonnet-in-progress at ten lines is not a sonnet yet. Nonetheless, partworks are crucially distinct from *mere* non-artworks of the quotidian kind (i.e., ordinary objects). Artistic effort has gone into bringing partworks toward a state of completion, and so less work needs to be done on them to complete the envisioned work. An unfinished sonnet is not simply a marked up piece of paper or ordinary bit of text. At ten lines, a sonnet-in-progress needs only four more, which would require rather less work than starting afresh. Intuitions may differ on whether a completeness requirement for art is appropriate, but it seems undeniable that, however much composition and sculpting went into them, Schubert's *"Unfinished"* Symphony is not a symphony, nor Michelangelo's *Atlas* a sculpture. It appears likewise unavoidable to acknowledge how very different the *"Unfinished"* is from ordinary sound, how different *Atlas* is from ordinary rock. Locating partworks thus on the cusp between art and non-art seems like the only reasonable thing to do.

2

At this point it should be apparent that at least one desideratum of art theories is the ability to allow and account for the partial status of partworks. Arguably a theory of art should be able to do this, and certainly not in an ad hoc manner. If an art theory proves unequal to this task, this will count as a serious mark against the theory. Even if a theory provides otherwise reasonable criteria for distinguishing art from non-art, such explanatory failure will remain a shortcoming, undermining any claim it might have to overall classificatory success. A surprising thing about most contemporary art theories is that they appear woefully inadequate in allowing much less accounting for partworks as such. Most if not all of these theories implicitly adhere to a rigidly dichotomous, all-or-nothing perspective that leaves no real cusp for partworks.

Institutional theories hold, roughly, that it is both necessary and sufficient for art that a thing be an artefact and be presented as a candidate for appreciation to the artworld, or that the artefact have artwork status conferred on it by someone acting on behalf of the artworld.[2] Such a view finds partworks difficult to accommodate. Take the presentation view first. An unfinished sculpture like *Bearded Slave*, though incomplete, is certainly an artefact, and it has been offered to the artworld as a candidate for appreciation. This is sufficient, on a naïve presentation view, for *Bearded Slave* to count as a full-blown sculptural artwork. But it is not one. (I assume here that the piece is not offered as an odd form of found art, though perhaps in principle it could be, in which case it would still not count as a finished sculpture.) On the status conferral view, the unfinished sculpture, though an artefact, presumably has not, owing to its unfinished state, had artwork status conferred on it by someone acting on behalf of the artworld. If someone were to, or were to try to, confer such status, he or she would produce, if anything, short of chiselling out the rest, the peculiar form of found art mentioned above. Claiming that partial art status can be conferred on behalf of the artworld seems ad hoc, and increases just suspicion that institutional theories leave something crucial out of the mix. The act of status conferral in cases of traditional art is sometimes thought to be an implicit matter of making the work. However implausible this might seem, given that status conferral in general is an explicit, formal, all-or-nothing matter, it is doubly implausible to suggest that partial artwork status is implicitly conferred unconsciously by an artist's partial completion of a work. Neither can account for partworks: the presentation view inflates, where the status conferral view deflates, the partial status of partworks. (I have glossed

---

[2]See George Dickie, *The Art Circle* (New York: Haven Publications, 1984), 80–81; *Art and the Aesthetic: An Institutional Analysis* (Ithaca, NY : Cornell U Press, 1974), 34.

over certain details here to cut a wider swath of institution-theoretic possibilities: for instance, Dickie's presentation view requires that an artefact be of a *kind* created for artworld presentation, but on the status conferral view it is only a *set* of an artefact's aspects on which art status will be conferred. My main point is unaffected by either gloss. If partworks are not of a kind created for artworld presentation, then they count, on the refined presentation account, as mere non-artworks, just as on the status conferral view.)

According to historical theories, what makes something art now is bearing a certain kind of relation to art of the past, typically by being intended to be regarded in one of the ways art of the past has been correctly regarded.[3] (I use 'artefact' here rather than the more-inclusive 'thing,' as I do with Beardsley's preferred phrase, 'arrangement of conditions', for ease of exposition.) Partworks present a double challenge here. There seems to be good reason to suppose that it is not partworks themselves that are ever intended to be regarded in a historically permissible way, but rather the finished works that partworks were intended to become, which leaves partworks merely non-artworks of the quotidian kind. On the other hand, if a partwork is itself (as part of the envisioned work) intended to be so regarded, it either counts as a stand-alone artwork (which may be the case sometimes), or more forcefully fits the historical criterion and counts, where it should not count, as a full-blown artwork.

Aesthetic theories are similarly challenged by partworks. On the intentionalist view, it is necessary and sufficient for art that an artefact be deliberately created so as to provide aesthetic experience or reward aesthetic attention.[4] Again, in the case of partworks, the object of the intent is not the partwork itself but the envisioned finished work that the partwork is becoming, which relegates partworks, again, to non-art of the quotidian kind. In the case that the partwork itself is (sometimes, though often not) the object of such intent, we have once more either a stand-alone artwork, or a partwork counting as full-blown art where it ought not to. Aesthetically appealing partworks, such as all of those mentioned above, will prove straightforward counterexamples to functionalist theories,[5] since they are artefacts that reliably provoke

---

[3] Jerrold Levinson, "Refining Art Historically," *Journal of Aesthetics and Art Criticism* 47 (1989): 21.

[4] For example, Monroe C. Beardsley, "An Aesthetic Definition of Art," in *What Is Art?*, ed. Hugh Curtler (New York: Haven, 1983), 19.

[5] For example, George Schlesinger, "Aesthetic Experience and the Definition of Art," *British Journal of Aesthetics* 19 (1979): 175.

aesthetic experience and yet should not be counted, as functionalism would count them, as full-blown artworks.

Related problems face various anti-essentialist theories of art. Functional-institutional, historical-functional,[6] and other such hybrid views inherit the same problems besetting each of their constituent theoretical sources, and for obvious reasons. The family resemblance view of artworks, along with more recent cluster-theoretic accounts,[7] will also find partworks to pose a real challenge. For instance, it is not clear why unfinished Michelangelos, which resemble his finished sculptures much more so than most sculptures do, would not count as artworks, to say nothing of the tight relational similarities between the two types. If, however, such partworks might be foisted out of the full-blown artwork class, then they will be unduly relegated, once again, to the class of mere non-artworks of the quotidian kind. A resemblance/cluster-theoretic account already faces tough resemblance cases, but if partworks do, as it seems they do, lie on the cusp between what is and is not art, these problems grow to unwieldy proportions.

3

The inability of much current aesthetic theory to do justice to partworks highlights the need to reorient the theory of art at a fundamental level. The first step should be diagnosis, figuring out what has gone, if not completely wrong, then at least not completely right either. In most of the theories discussed above, the link between an artefact— whether artwork or partwork—and the artmaking conditions posited (institutional, historical, intentional, functional, or resemblance) does not provide the wherewithal to disambiguate partworks from artworks, or from mere non-art, in any plausible way. Part of the problem seems to be excessive focus on the link between already existing artefacts and whatever is deemed the art transfiguring relation, where the focus rather should also include (when relevant) what goes into producing the artefact, that is, the link between creators and the works they bring into being. To characterize this link exclusively in terms of transfigu-

---

[6]See, respectively, Stephen Davies, *Definitions of Art* (Ithaca: Cornell U Press, 1991), 207–21; Robert Stecker, *Artworks: Definition, Meaning, Value* (University Park: Pennsylvania State U Press, 1997), 48–65.

[7]For example, Berys Gaut, "'Art' as a Cluster Concept," in *Theories of Art Today*, ed. Noël Carroll (Madison: U of Wisconsin Press, 2000), 25–44.

ration, artefactual production, or even artefactual production spurred by post-production intentions (correct regard, aesthetic experience) seems insufficient, for the object of the intent is the work that may emerge, not its partwork predecessors. What we need is a graded concept, one the application of which admits of degrees, putting partworks in league with things that are partly bald, parboiled, somewhat grey, or mildly depressing. Work is a graded concept, in that one can do work to varying degrees. But work is not the concept we need, it is rather the concept of which we need to give an account.

Artefactuality is of no use here, because partworks count as full-blown artefacts, although not complete as intended, much less as full-blown art. That is the received view, at any rate. It should be noted, however, that a graded notion of artefactuality might be proposed. Whatever the motivations for such a graded concept of artefactuality—partefactuality, as it were—the implications are untenable. Artefactual degrees would depend upon how much work goes into the production of a given artefact. Thus we could have two artefacts completely alike in every respect (appearance, constitution, and function), yet have radically different orders of artefactuality, one, for instance, being two or a thousand times *more* of an artefact than the other. But there are no degrees of *being made*. The scepticism that would ensue vis-à-vis the application of the concept of artefactuality, which is, if not essentially defined by, at least intimately tied to, the task of sorting into types the various things we find in the world, undercuts whatever ground might be gained otherwise. Such gradations in the concept of artefactuality are, by implication, simply untenable.

A much more promising possibility for marshalling a gradable concept in service of understanding the link between artists and the works they create is to appeal, not to the mere production of artefacts, but to ways in which such production is often characterized in more traditional aesthetic theory. One obvious candidate is the concept of expression, of artistic creation as an expressive act. (Among the various accounts of artistic creation as a form of expression, the classic is of course Collingwood's.[8]) Although expressivist theories are fraught with many difficulties (especially where it is only the expression of emotion that is deemed relevant), nothing prevents contemporary theory from borrowing from such accounts as needed without wholeheartedly endorsing or capitulating to them. An expressive act creates mean-

---

[8]R.G. Collingwood, *The Principles of Art* (Oxford: Oxford U Press, 1938), 109–44.

ing (creates a meaningful item) in a way that satisfies the immediate impulse to do so, whatever further ends may be sought. Ordinary actions and utterances are expressive in a rather weak sense: one can make psychological inferences from a person's behaviour. Artworks are psychologically revealing too, and often yield general descriptions or explanations of their "messages." But paraphrasing the meaning of ordinary actions and utterances at best leaves out nothing essential. With art, though, attempts to paraphrase might be better or worse, helpful or hindering, but must, even at best, omit the essential particularity of what is/how it is expressed in the work.

We may characterize the expressive act of artmaking as an attempt to realize a vision—a perspective that, though intuitive, implies a perhaps uncomfortable realism about artistic vision, although it does not presuppose naïvely that an artwork must be somehow fully blueprinted in every last detail in the artist's consciousness before any work begins. The process of creation is not blind, of course, but nor is it usually fully foreseen. Much can be discovered, worked out, experimented with, and revised as the work proceeds. Perhaps an artist's vision can only be fully discerned, even by the artist, in its complete realization in the actual finished work. This view is hardly a novel one. Even when a work is finished, and has been signed off on by the artist, accounting fully for what makes the work a satisfactory realization of the vision may elude its progenitor, apart from an intuitive sense that the effort has sufficed. Even if the work is seen, after the fact, as constitutive of what was expressed in the creative process, the work remains answerable to the purposes that initially prompted the creative process and guided it to completion. As Merleau-Ponty remarks on seeing Matisse paint a brushstroke: "[T]he stroke was chosen so as to satisfy ten conditions scattered on the painting, unformulated and unformulable for anyone other than Matisse, since they were defined and imposed only by the intention to make *this particular painting which did not yet exist*" (emphasis in original).[9] A vision not only motivates but constrains the work that elaborates it.

The graded character of expression is reflected in ordinary descriptions, apropos of unfinished artworks, of incomplete expressive acts in

---

[9]Maurice Merleau-Ponty, *The Prose of the World*, ed. Claude Lefort, trans. John O'Neill (Evanston: Northwestern U Press, 1973), 44–45. For a different interpretation, see Sue Campbell, *Interpreting the Personal: Expression and the Formation of Feelings* (Ithaca: Cornell U Press, 1997), 50–51. It is interesting to note, as Campbell does, that Merleau-Ponty left *The Prose of the World* unfinished.

the weaker, ordinary sense. We often speak of not fully expressing our thoughts, of revealing only part of what we feel, or of leaving our point half made. In such cases, an expressive act has been initiated and perhaps continued, but it has not been concluded. If we can characterize artistic creation as an expressive act of some kind—an expression of self, of vision, of mental states—then we have a straightforward explanation of partworks as the products of only partly completed expressive acts. The shortfall between partwork and art is explained by, and corresponds to, a partwork's degree of expressive incompleteness, that is, the extent to which the vision that motivates and constrains the work remains unrealized. To be clear, the proposal offered is not that an expressive link between creator and work is sufficient for art, but rather that this link might be necessary, particularly if this move allows us to account for the status of partworks as such. There is plenty of room for other necessary conditions (institutional, historical, aesthetic, and so on), however radically this might alter the shape and spirit of such views.

In a sense, then, what I am offering here is a threshold view of art, though one distinct from other sorts of threshold view found in aesthetic theory. By saying this I do not mean, for instance, that a work, in order to count as art, has to achieve a certain level of aesthetic value, audience approval, or critical endorsement. Rather, I am proposing an expressivist view of the unremarkable fact that in most cases of creating art, the work proceeds incrementally until the job is done and the artist signs off on it, which signifies that the expressive act is complete. (In fact, we can interpret the sign off as the summary expressive act announcing that everything else has been done—a sort of meta-expressive "That's all.") Relative to the envisioned final product, in-process work is expressive only in part, just as water approaching the boiling point, though not boiling yet, is still heating up. Vis-à-vis the respective thresholds of boiling point and finished state, gradations of temperature and expression allow for plausible and theoretically useful descriptions of heating up and creating out.

4

If trying to preserve an intuitive view of partworks as occupying a middle ground between non-artworks of the quotidian kind and bona fide artworks has such drastic theoretical consequences as I have suggested above, then this might be taken as a reductio of the intuitive view. Perhaps then we may be motivated to deny that there can, strictly speaking, be partworks at all, to avail ourselves in other words of either an inflationary strategy (elevating partworks to the status of full-blown art) or a deflationary strategy (reducing partworks to the status of mere non-art). In fact, though I have called the view of partworks proposed here intuitive, no doubt there will be competing intuitions that point to one or the other of these strategies.

The inflationary strategy implies rejecting the completeness requirement for art: where a work is unfinished, it may still count as art, even if the artist has not signed off on it. One might be tempted toward this strategy by the tendency to count unfinished art as part of an artist's *body of work*, by the superficial grammar of such phrases as 'unfinished work', and so on. One might also find the inflationary strategy plausible in cases of "near-miss" partworks, such as *The Trial*, in which the gaps are either unnoticed or easily filled in by the reader. Such differences between artworks and near-miss partworks are perhaps indeed negligible in this phenomenological sense. However, while it may be appropriate to include partworks within an artist's body of work, this does not imply proper inclusion in a list of the artist's works (for which completeness might be needed), since 'work' in 'body of work' operates as a mass noun requiring neither discreteness nor completion of the object's constituents, whereas this is not obviously so for 'work of art' in the usual sense. Likewise, we should not be misled into thinking that 'unfinished' in 'unfinished artwork' operates like an ordinary predicate, as in 'representational artwork', but should instead note that it is rather more like 'interrupted sentence', which does not properly refer to sentences, only sentence fragments. Although the inflationary strategy is somewhat plausible for near-miss partworks, it fails to be so for cases of glaring incompleteness, such "manifest" partworks as the *"Unfinished" Symphony*, and so on.

The inflationary strategy also gives rise to *sorites* problems, for if *Atlas* counts as a full-blown sculpture, then so must earlier and earlier stages of it, right back to the first chisel stroke on the original hunk of marble. The untouched marble might have counted as found art, and the once-struck block might have counted as a sculpture—in another context. But barring the freeing of statue from stone in a single chisel stroke, the un- or barely touched marble does not count as a sculpture when intended to become *David* or the sculpture *Atlas* never was. One might simply insist that *Atlas* is in no sense less a work than *David* is, citing perhaps the fact that (as with *Requiem* or the *"Unfinished"*), incompleteness aside, such partworks are substantial enough to provide rich aesthetic rewards, and so ought to count as artworks no less than a vast majority of artistically inferior finished works. But of course providing for aesthetic experience, intense and profound as it might be, is insufficient for art, and so the undeniable quality of a great partwork will not make it an artwork.

Still, if the inflationary strategy were to succeed, the theoretical implications of *prima facie* partworks would remain significant. For instance, partworks are *not*, as a kind, intended either to be presented to an artworld public, to be regarded as past art has correctly been, or to provide for aesthetic experience. Thus the inflationary strategy casts *prima facie* partworks as counterexamples to prominent varieties of institutional, historical, and aesthetic theories, since *qua* artworks they do not meet the posited criteria. The deflationary strategy likewise serves up partworks as counterexamples, since *qua* non-art they are nonetheless artefacts presented to the artworld as candidates for appreciation, intended (by curators rather than artists) to be regarded in historically appropriate ways, and providing for aesthetic experience.

The deflationary strategy of reducing partworks to mere non-art perhaps seems plausible in that, aside from the work remaining to be done, the artist has not signed off, and what crucial cases like Duchamp's *Fountain* are supposed to show is that it is (virtually) sufficient for art to have an artist sign off on *something*. This signatory condition is the one procedural requirement for art on which various theoretical approaches might comfortably agree. Even if one could sign off on a work on the artist's or the artworld's behalf, both the unfinished status of the work and the lack of artist's signatory closure suggests that whatever the artwork we "create" or "finish" by presentation or status conferral *cannot* be either the envisioned work or properly the artist's. We cannot make the *"Unfinished" Symphony* a symphony just by signing off on it, nor would it be Schubert's if we either pulled a Süssmayr or somehow transfigured the *"Unfinished"* into a finished musical or perhaps meta-musical work of another kind, just as it is Duchamp and not a plumbing manufacturer who is the artist of *Fountain*.

Insisting that the signatory move is the *only* stage of artmaking that ever matters simply ignores the undeniable importance of work already done on partworks and the substantial work required to bring most types of art into being. Often an artist has not signed off *because* there is work yet to be done. Putting the 'work' back in 'artwork' does not, however, rule out cases like *Fountain*, virtually effortless and instantaneous as its transfiguration might have been. In these cases we might have a kind of instant artmaking, where the work is initiated and completed in a single act, artworks without any precedent partworks. Be that as it may. The point is not that all artworks were partworks first; perhaps substantial work is necessary, not for all forms of art, but for most. The point is rather that partworks as such have important implications for theories of art. Better to explain fringe cases like *Fountain* in terms of more standard cases, if possible, than to let the fringe rule unfettered over the entire artwork class. Since most if not all artworks were partworks at some point, the intuitive view of partworks offered here accommodates such fringe cases without straying too far from art at its very core.

2 A COMPREHENSIVIST THEORY OF ART

Matthew Lipman once remarked that many theories of art focus too narrowly on one or another aspect of the aesthetic process and, as a result, inhibit the understanding of that process as a whole.[1] On the basis of this complaint I shall call Lipman the founder of comprehensivism, by which I mean the view that art must be understood holistically, neither the artist, the artwork, nor the audience being excluded from an overall conception. My purpose here is to outline a definition of art in strict adherence to this view. To do so, I will have to give an account both of what artists do in creating artwork and of what happens to audiences in experiencing it. As any such account must in some sense be psychological in character, it seems natural to begin with a sketch, however rough, of the mind.

Mental states, no matter what ontological status one reserves for them, divide roughly into two broad categories. On the one hand there are beliefs, assumptions, doubts, conjectures, predictions, and so forth, which may be called intellectual states. On the other there are desires, hopes, fears, sorrows, anxieties, and so forth, which may be called emotional states. One reason for accepting this distinction, apart from its intuitive appeal, is that intellectual states embed propositional or otherwise representational content, while some emotional states do not. Whereas one can be depressed or happy or anxious without being depressed or happy or anxious about anything, one cannot believe or doubt or predict without believing or doubting or predicting some-

---

[1] M. Lipman, *What Happens in Art* (New York: Meredith, 1967), p. 15. See also W. Crazier and P. Greenhalgh, 'The Empathy Principle: Towards a Model for the Psychology of Art', *Journal for the Theory of Social Behaviour*, Vol. 22, 1992, pp. 63-79.

thing. Another way of putting this is that some emotional states can be freefloating, that is, unattached to specific contents. Not all emotional states are of this character, however; one presumably cannot desire without desiring something. But desires and beliefs have different directions of fit.[2] A belief is true when its content maps onto the world, while a desire is fulfilled when the world comes to map onto the desire's content. Intellectual states such as entertaining and wondering have no direction of fit and thus share this in common with emotional states such as sorrow and pleasure. But emotional states of this sort are complex in a way that entertaining and wondering are not. Entertaining a thought is simply to entertain it, while being sorry that, say, something happened involves a belief that it happened and a wish that it had not.

Cursory as they might be, the above remarks should illustrate that distinguishing between intellect and emotion is not inapt. Still, it would be unwise to suppose that this distinction constitutes a dichotomy, since there are some mental states (even setting aside the purely phenomenal aspects of experience) that do not fit neatly into either category. Convictions, and perhaps intuitions as well, seem more or less to be belief-like states invested with emotion. Further, as we have seen, some emotional states contain as essential elements certain intellectual states. The interaction across categories suggested by these cases is mirrored by the gross anatomy of the brain, as is the distinction on which this interaction depends. The higher cortex is intellectual and reflective, the diencephalon emotional and appetitive, the tissue between the two largely integrative in function. Both the mind's scope and limits, it has been argued, stem from a nearly constant conflict between the diencephalon and higher cortex.[3] In intentional terms this amounts to three kinds of tension: that between inconsistent contents, as when I believe I should do one thing but want to do something else; that between states with the same content, as when I doubt that something is the case but wish it to be so; and that between intellectual states and freefloating emotions, as when I suppose there is nothing to be anxious about but am anxious nonetheless.

---

[2]This is Searle's term. Some of what I say here is to be found in J.R. Searle, *Intentionality* (Cambridge: Cambridge U. P., 1983), pp. 1-2, 7-8. Searle does not explicitly emphasize the distinction that I do, though he might well have done.

[3]See A.T. Simeons, *Man's Presumptuous Brain* (New York: Dutton, 1961), *passim.* For reasons why such an approach is viable, see C.A. Mace, 'Psychology and Aesthetics' in H. Osborne (ed.), *Aesthetics in the Modern World* (London: Thames and Hudson, 1968), p. 285.

In applying this sketch of the mind to the problem of artistic creation, it should be clear that the sort of intentionality that concerns us is distinct from that commonly held to be at issue in the literature.[4] What an artist intends to express in an artwork is less crucial to my analysis than the intentional form of many of the mental states that eventuate in the production of artwork. And so I will bracket debates that centre on the artist's intentions. But by so doing I do not mean to marginalize the importance of these debates, and offer as a default position that such intentions are largely irrelevant to the interpretation of artwork,[5] and that there are varying degrees to which intentions delimit and determine artistic expression.[6] In addition, I will focus more on analyzing expression itself than on justifying the already plausible notion that the creation of artwork is in some sense expressive.

An act of expression, understood broadly, is such that there is someone who performs it and something they express by performing it. Expression is at once expression *by* and *of*. For example, when someone says of Mozart's *Requiem* that it is moving, an opinion about the *Requiem* is expressed, and the speaker has done something, i.e. uttered a sentence, to express it. It does not matter so much whether the speaker must express the opinion in order to hold it, as some might claim, or whether it is possible simply to hold it without expressing it. What does matter is that the opinion can be expressed in various ways, or in the same way repeatedly, by contextually appropriate facial expressions or applause, by uttering or writing down the right words, and so on. That what is expressible at all is capable of being expressed more than once means that an act of expression consists, partly if not fully, in tokening what is expressed.

Normally we understand expression as something one can do to oneself or to others, as the opiner may express her opinion to her-

---

[4]For recent discussions of this sort of intentionality, see S. Feagin, 'On Defining and Interpreting Art Intentionalistically', *British Journal of Aesthetics,* Vol. 22, 1982, pp. 65-77; J. Duran, 'Collingwood and Intentionality', *British Journal of Aesthetics,* Vol. 27, 1987, pp. 32-38; S. Davies, 'A Note on Feagin on Interpreting Art Intentionalistically', *British Journal of Aesthetics,* Vol. 27, 1987, pp. 178-180; D. Kolak, 'Art and Intentionality', *Journal of Aesthetics and Art Criticism,* Vol. 48, 1990, pp. 158-162; and L. Calhoun, 'The Intentional Fallacy', *Philosophy and Literature,* Vol. 18, 1994, pp. 337-338.

[5]B. Vermazen, 'Expression as Expression', *Pacific Philosophical Quarterly,* Vol. 67, 1986, p. 202.

[6]V.A. Howard, 'Expression as Hands-on Construction', *Journal of Aesthetic Education,* Vol. 22, 1988, pp. 134-135.

self or, say, to other appreciators of music. The latter sort is the more aesthetically interesting, as it can take verbal, written, gestural, pictorial, symbolic, coded, or any number of forms in isolation or in combination, and as such is worth characterizing more precisely. The expression involved in the creation of art is of the latter kind, expressing to others, and in the sense that creation culminates in the finished artwork—the sculptor leaves behind a sculpture, the novelist a novel, the painter a painting, and so on—the act of expression can be seen as the objectification of what is expressed.[7] This is not to say that artistic creation must occasion objects in the narrow sense, for this would unduly exclude performance and situationist art from the artwork class. Rather, artistic expression occasions objects in the broad sense, including performances and situations, that are accessible to and scrutinizable by the public, at least in principle.[8]

There is an obstacle to holding that artistic creation is the objectification of expression, and that is an ambiguity in 'expression', which can refer either to what is expressed or to the act of expressing it. If what is expressed is a mental state, then in many cases we can speak either of the state itself or of its content as the expression which is objectified, and the act of expression as what, through tokening it in the right way, objectifies it. As the objective mark of such an expressive act simply is the artwork, we can also speak of the act itself as being objectified in the work; it is both of these senses that I want the phrase 'objectified expression' to capture. The extent to which objectification is successful is the extent to which its product satisfies, for whatever reasons, the desire to express the mental states that gave rise to it. I mean to suggest by this that such satisfaction is all there is to a product's being the objectification of the mental states causally contributory to its production. Even in the allographic arts an artwork's production and the mental states causally contributory thereto, however intricate and protracted the causal pathway may be, are both objectified in the work. And they are objectified insofar as either the work or, in the case of a score or script, the prescription for

---

[7]C.J. Ducasse, *The Philosophy of Art* (New York: Dover, 1966), p. 112.

[8]The proviso 'in principle' is crucial. Many artists produce artwork without it ever, or without the intent of it ever, achieving public presentation. This, I think, does damage to many institutional theories of art. See G. Dickie, 'The Institutional Conception of Art' in B.R. Tilghman (ed.), *Language and Aesthetics* (Kansas: University Press of Kansas, 1973), pp. 21-30. One can reject such views, however, without giving up the notion that the character of art is social. See N. Carroll, 'Art, Practice, and Narrative', *The Monist,* Vol. 71, 1988, pp. 140-166.

its performance satisfies the artist in this minimal way.

Of course it does not follow that these mental states are palpably present, much less recognizable, in the artwork itself. Questions about what is expressed by Bach's F-minor Concerto, if they can be posed at all, are pretty much opaque to both careful analysis of the music and conjecture, well- or ill-informed, as to what was either on Bach's mind when he composed it or in the minds of the musicians who performed it. That expression can be objectified irrevocably incognito, in some artforms more obviously than in some others, is partly why minimal constraints should be placed on what counts as objectification. As to what kinds of mental state can be objectified in artwork, I see no reason to be restrictive. Intellectual and emotional intentional states, their contents, and freefloating emotions may all, in various combinations and orderings, find expression in art.[9] To indicate what strictures, if any, should be placed on this multitude requires a shift of attention from artistic creation to aesthetic experience, or in other words from the effective to the affective.

The sketch of the mind with which this paper began leads to an interesting conception of aesthetic experience. Art is valuable in part because acquaintance with it does something for the acquainted. If the view that aesthetic experience is more harmonious than chaotic, more symphonic than cacophonic,[10] is at all convincing, then it seems that art elicits experiences unlike those that typify mental life generally. Experiences of this sort are not conflictual but resolutive. In neuroanatomical terms this resolution is a cessation of conflict between the diencephalon and higher cortex. In psychological terms it is a mitigation of tension between occurrent intellectual and emotional mental states: inconsistent contents enter into higher order resolution, as when the belief that Othello will kill Desdemona and the desire that he not do so are cohered by a sense of tragedy; antagonism between states with the same or similar content is suspended, as when the belief and fear that Othello will commit murder do not issue in the crowd's rushing the stage to prevent it; freefloating emotions latch onto whatever best corrals them, as when one's general despair at the denouement of *Othello* falls under the concept of unfortunate desert.

---

[9]Fragments of this view are suggested in J. Hospers, 'The Concept of Artistic Expression' in J. Hospers (ed.), *Introductory Readings in Aesthetics* (New York: Free Press, 1969), p. 145, Vermazen, op. cit., p 201, and W. Shibles, 'Humanistic Art', *Critical Review*, Vol. 8, 1994, pp. 371-392.

[10]I.A. Richards et al., *The Foundations of Aesthetics* (London: Allen & Unwin, 1925), p. 76.

It should be emphasized that this resolution is not a quelling of either intellectual or emotional responses but rather a coherent engagement of both. In this way aesthetic experience is unlike base pleasure and detached abstraction, which amount to prescinding in the first case from the intellect and in the second from the emotions.

This notion of aesthetic experience tells us something about artistic creation. Once we realize that the creative process must be sustained in order for it to culminate in a finished artwork, it becomes clear that what sustains this process is the artists' appreciation, however inchoate, of the work they are bringing to fruition.[11] Since appreciation of artwork depends on experiencing it *as* artwork, part of the sustaining cause of its production is the artist's resolutive experience of what the expressive act is coming to objectify. This is not to restrict the mental states which can be objectified in artwork to those which are relata of resolution. Rather, any number of mental states are objectifiable in artwork provided there is a mediate resolution between the impetus for and result of their expression. The point is that resolution in the subject of aesthetic experience does not require, and should not be confused with, resolution in its object. The conclusion to *The Sun Also Rises,* for instance, lacks closure. But this irresolution is one without which the book would be vastly inferior.

Before moving on, I should distinguish this account from certain historical and contemporary alternatives. When Nietzsche speaks of 'the excitement of the hearer which is Apollonian as well as Dionysian',[12] one might suppose that Apollo is to be taken as an icon of the intellect, Dionysus as an icon of the emotions. This would be hasty, for Nietzsche takes the Apollonian to subsume light, dream, and reflection, the Dionysian dark, primevum, and instinct,[13] which cuts across my distinction. Santayana maintains that aesthetic experience is a mingling of sensory and perceptive pleasures. It would be odd to construe sensory pleasures as emotional and perceptive pleasures as intellectual, but were we to do so it should be pointed out that, for Santayana, the first kind of pleasure is prior to and requisite for the second, and each is a pleasure in its own right.[14] Aesthetic experience on my account is not a mingling of pleasures but, if you will, a pleasure

---

[11]Lipman, op. cit., p. 15; Vermazen, op. cit., p. 201.

[12]F. Nietzsche in W. Kaufman (trans.), *The Birth of Tragedy* (New York: Vintage, 1967), p. 132. This is a deliberate misquotation from Kaufman. Why? 'Apollonian' rings more Apollonian than 'Apollinian'.

[13]Ibid., Sections 1-5, 21 and elsewhere.

[14]G. Santayana, *The Sense of Beauty* (New York: Dover, 1955), p. 46.

of mingling, and there need be no priority of one mingled element to another. Roger Scruton takes aesthetic experience to contain intellectual states, such as belief, as well as noncognitive phenomena of the imagination.[15] By contrast, I emphasize the emotional nature of aesthetic experience. At the same time I do not deny that the imagination of the experiencer can contribute to their experience. Salient features of an artwork are interpreted, frequently by trial and error, such that the interpretation coheres with, and shapes to coherence, the elements of the experience pertinent to them. Granted, these remarks are a bit perfunctory. They are not, however, peremptory.

Now that the groundwork has been laid, I should like to propose, at least in outline form, a comprehensivist theory of art, the materials for which are the accounts of artistic creation and aesthetic experience achieved thus far. Artists objectify expression. Artworks are the objectification of that expression. Audiences experience that expression resolutively.[16] The problem is that these aspects hang together in a way that does not mandate a univocal formulation in natural language. We can define art in terms of either the complex relation between artist, artwork, and audience, the process uniting the three, the object of aesthetic experience, or the subject of aesthetic experience. It would be arbitrary to follow only one of these tacks, but since art is readily identified in ordinary language with particular artworks, it is the third that I shall highlight. *Art is objectified expression elicitive of resolutive experience.* More precisely, x is art if and only if x is objectified expression and x elicits resolutive experience. Notice that this definition allows for the possibility that the same individual can be both artist and audience. Notice too that x may be instantiated by anything over which one can quantify, object or event, and into which one can objectify expression.

One of the nice implications of this proposal is that the concepts of artist, artwork, and audience are apodoses to the concept of art, not protases. Someone is an artist only if their expression is objectified into something that elicits resolutive experience. Similarly, something is an artwork only if it is objectified expression elicitive of resolutive

---

[15]R. Scruton, *Art and Imagination* (London: Methuen, 1974), p. 83.

[16]It has been argued that psychological definitions of art are inadequate. See D.J. Dempster, 'Aesthetic Experience and Psychological Definitions of Art', *Journal of Aesthetics and Art Criticism,* Vol. 4, 1985, pp. 153-165. While I agree that merely psychological definitions of art are inadequate, a theory of art that incorporates aesthetic experience must, on pain of vacuousness, make reference to the psychological.

experience.[17] Aesthetic experience is likewise insufficient for the experiencer to qualify as an audience, sufficiency depending on whether the experience is elicited by objectified expression. Each aspect of the aesthetic situation is therefore as dependent on the completeness of that situation as the situation is on it.

Consider the following cases. Suppose a lump of marble found in nature resembles Michelangelo's *David* exactly. Although its phenomenal properties are identical to those of *David,* it is not a statue, for it lacks the relational property of having come from an artist. Or again, suppose a vandal throws a brick through a window. We call the police. A situationist throws the same brick in the same way through the same window. We applaud. One difference is that the situationist elicits resolutive experience while the vandal does not, even though both could be said to objectify expression in breaking the window. Another is that the situationist, unlike the vandal, does not really objectify expression in the breaking of the window but rather in the situation of so doing in front of an audience convened for that purpose. Certainly the vandal might implore comrades to bear witness to the destruction, and their witnessing might in fact be resolutive. In cases of appropriate civil disobedience, and so forth, we might not be loath to consider an act of vandalism as possessing artistic quality. I think it highly unlikely that witnessing an act of pure vandalism could really be resolutive. But if it could, it would be presumptuous to allow an excessive elitism to rule it out of the artwork class altogether, since where aesthetics fails criticism can take up most of the slack.

Another implication is that art is in part a verdictive notion, since artwork is indexed to those who experience it resolutively. Objectified expression, in other words, must be found artistic in order to be artistic. There may be cases where objectified expression counts as artwork despite disputes about whether these cases should be so counted. On my proposal the resolutive experience of anyone confers art status on the objectified expression that elicits it.[18] It does not follow from this, though, that my proposal is relativistic. Art is dependent on but not

---

[17]This obviates Wollheim's linkage problem. See R. Wollheim, *Art and Its Objects* (New York: Harper & Row, 1971), p. 29. One makes sense of the links by making sense of the linkage, not vice versa.

[18]It should be apparent that my view straddles proceduralist and functionalist aesthetic theories, although of the two trends I am more closely affiliated with the latter. By doing so I need not place excessive procedural constraints on the concept of art. For more on this see S. Davies, *Definitions of Art* (Ithaca: Cornell U. P., 1990), pp. 1-3.

determined by individual verdicts, for there are constraints on what counts as art independent of such verdicts. I may encounter objectified expression without at all having a resolutive experience of it, yet I can still speak of it as an artwork, since others have experienced it as such.

Nor does it follow that aesthetics and art criticism should be unilaterally segregated. In one sense I would have criticism give aesthetics as wide a berth as possible. To derive standards of what art ought to be from conceptions of what it is, it seems, is to commit the naturalistic fallacy. However, the two are intimately connected. When it comes to interpreting artwork, or to deciding what sorts of thing merit aesthetic attention, critics are the experts to whom some measure of deference is owed. Limiting this deference is necessary because, if my view of artistic creation is right, interpretations of artwork can be better or worse than others, but not canonical.[19] I am not claiming that the occurrence of resolutive experience is more important than the way it is elicited. Nor am I claiming that the concept of art is nonevaluative. For the most part I have explored art's merely descriptive aspects, leaving the prescriptive and the relations between it and the descriptive for those more sensitive to the task.[20]

---

[19]If pushed on this point, I should refer the reader to D.C. Dennett, *The Intentional Stance* (Cambridge: MIT Press, 1987), *passim*. Dennett argues on Quinean grounds that there are no 'deep' facts about the content of anything meaningful, mental states, utterances, or what have you. The same goes for art.

[20]For their helpful comments and criticisms I would like to thank the Editor, the reviewers, Steven Burns, R.M. Martens, K. Brad Wray, Kevin de Laplante, Tim Kenyon, Marc Ramsay, and Larry Holt. An earlier version of this paper was presented in August 1994 to a colloquium at Dalhousie University. To those who participated I also give thanks.

3

THE MARGINAL LIFE OF THE AUTHOR

Though somewhat difficult to untangle, the death of the author thesis (DOA) is both provocative and important. Apart from certain critical analyses, however, it has not been given due attention from analytic philosophers. In this chapter I will defend DOA from an analytic perspective. I will argue that Barthes and Foucault are more or less right, though not for the reasons they think they are.

The ironies surrounding DOA may tempt one to ignore it as simply another postmodern indulgence. For one, the champions of DOA themselves avoidably fail to marginalize authors in the manner they prescribe. In "The Death of the Author," Barthes dubs his central example, an excerpt from Balzac's "Sarrasine," the *Balzac* sentence.[1] In "What Is an Author?" Foucault makes sure to cite Beckett's "What does it matter who's speaking?" as *Beckett's*.[2] Similarly, both credit Mallarmé with serving a pivotal role in the emergence, or re-emergence, of authorial self-suppression.[3] If authors are so unimportant as to deserve metaphorical death, why bother mentioning them? Why credit the poet himself rather than the poetry? As authors, Barthes and Foucault have enlarged their own importance by denying that of authors generally. They eschew reason, yet offer arguments for the eschewal. By assailing authorial privilege, they have further cemented, in cer-

---

[1] Roland Barthes, "The Death of the Author," in *Image-Music-Text*, trans. Stephen Heath (New York: Hill and Wang, 1977), p. 147 (hereafter DA); "La Morte de l'Auteur," *Manteia* 5 (1968): 16 (hereafter MA).

[2] Michel Foucault, "What Is an Author?" trans. Josué V. Harari, in Paul Rabinow, ed., *The Foucault Reader* (New York: Pantheon, 1984), p. 101 (hereafter WIA); "Qu'est-ce Qu'un Auteur?" *Bulletin de la Société Francaise de Philosophie* 63 (1969): 77 (hereafter QA).

[3] DA, p. 143; MA, p. 13; WIA, p. 105; QA, p. 79.

tain quarters at least, their own practically unassailable intellectual authority. The received view, by and large, has fostered not an explosion of creative interpretation but a sort of meaning nihilism, where delegitimation goes proxy for imaginative inquiry.[4] Telling as these ironies are, however, they do not bear on the defensibility of DOA, and this is the issue I will explore here.

I will begin by sorting out what DOA means and to what range of texts it applies. Following this, I will show how the arguments adduced for DOA by Barthes and Foucault are largely unsuccessful. Then I will develop a thought-experiment to the effect that while the content of authorial intentions is interpretively dispensable, the presumption of some intent or other is not. I will next offer an account of aesthetic meaning that allows for DOA as well as the disciplinary practice apparently threatened by it. My defense of DOA, then, will be somewhat limited, relegating the author not to the grave but to the margins. As it happens, more extreme measures in defense of DOA are neither necessary nor available.

What Is DOA?

Although DOA is never stated clearly and constitutes a nexus of many descriptive, normative, and epistemological questions, there are clues as to what the thesis amounts to. One such clue is the work the thesis is meant to do. It is supposed to liberate us from interpretively restrictive views of literature, views "tyrannically centred on the author,"[5] where the author is that "functional principle" that "impedes the free circulation, the free manipulation, the free composition, decomposition, and recomposition of fiction."[6] Both advocate freedom from the author, Barthes more narrowly in interpreting texts, Foucault more generally in what one *does* with texts, which a fortiori includes interpreting them. Notwithstanding legitimate moral qualms with Foucault's overarching vision, in which anonymous texts are written irresponsibly, appropriated indiscriminately, and distorted unconscionably, the central purpose of DOA, shared by its progenitors, is reader liberation in interpreting texts. Concerns about authorial rights and responsibili-

---

[4]Donald Keefer, "Reports of the Death of the Author," *Philosophy and Literature* 19 (1995): 81-82.

[5]DA, p. 143; MA, p. 13.

[6]WIA, p. 119; QA, p. 95.

ties, while important, are independent of this central purpose and its subserving thesis.

If the purpose of DOA is reader liberation, then the thesis should be designed to lift such constraints as untowardly limit that freedom, specifically, constraints on textual meaning. Such constraints allegedly inhere in conceiving of texts as authored, which artificially "closes" the writing, fixing the meaning of a text so that successively improved interpretations of it will univocally converge. It is to this idea of textual closure that the advocates of DOA stand fundamentally opposed. Barthes denies that a text is "a line of words releasing a single 'theological' meaning (the 'message' of the Author-god)."[7] Foucault makes the same point indirectly. "The author," he says, "is the principle of thrift in the proliferation of meaning," and once the author is removed, "fiction and its polysemous texts will once again function according to another mode,"[8] one presumably in which they are recognized *as* polysemous. Seán Burke writes: "[N]o longer reduced to a 'single message,' the text is opened to an unlimited variety of interpretations.... This is the message—indeed the 'single message'—of 'The Death of the Author.' "[9] None of the interpretations to which a text is open is de facto privileged, much less canonical, and so there is no such thing as *the* meaning of a text. As a result, textual meaning can, and furthermore should, proliferate. While one may reasonably doubt that the author's fatal wound is either a necessary or sufficient opening of the text, the thesis itself is, as I hope to show, defensible.

On a superficial level, DOA may seem mere approbation for the "new writing," from which the author self-consciously withdraws in a refusal to fix meaning and in defiance of literary conventions, a trend beginning at least with Mallarmé and arguably culminating in the *nouveau roman* of Robbe-Grillet. His novel *Djinn* is a striking illustration—one might say vindication—of DOA. In the fictional prologue, *Djinn* is presented as a text of which, despite the most thorough investigative efforts, nothing is known of the author. The purpose of the text is also unknown. Is it fiction? A dream journal? The diary of someone not quite sane? A manual for learning grammatical structure? The point is, it doesn't really matter. Our ignorance of such things does not preclude interpretation but rather promotes it.

---

[7]DA, p. 146; MA, p. 16.

[8]WIA, p. 119; QA, p. 95.

[9]Seán Burke, *The Death and Return of the Author: Criticism and Subjectivity in Barthes, Foucault and Derrida*, 2nd ed. (Edinburgh: Edinburgh University Press, 1998), p. 43.

The implication, it seems, is that where we have such information, we should not allow it to inhibit the proliferation of meaning in interpreting texts. It is not that authors of the *vieux roman* succeed in fixing meaning where they ought not to. Rather, they are mistaken to think they can, and disingenuous to pretend as much. DOA is meant to apply to literature broadly, and the new writing is to be lauded as a more honest and sanguine illustration of a thesis applying only inclusively to it.

Even so, it is not clear to what range of texts DOA applies. On the one hand, Barthes and Foucault draw examples almost exclusively from fiction, poetry, and plays, which suggests that DOA is meant to apply only to literary texts, that is, written art. Indeed, both often write as if this is precisely the range of texts they have in mind. On the other hand, Barthes claims that DOA collapses the distinction between literary and non-literary texts,[10] and Foucault holds that DOA covers all authored texts, including scientific and philosophical works.[11] But extending the scope of DOA beyond literary texts is less pressing than the issue of whether it applies to literary texts in the first place. Art seems to lend itself, more readily than anything else, to interpretive variance, and aesthetics tolerates this without scandal. But if texts are open to a variety, indeed, an *unlimited* variety of interpretations, does this mean that, in interpretive matters, anything goes? If it does, then we cannot plausibly maintain that DOA applies to non-literary texts, for these include "The Death of the Author" and "What Is an Author?" and we could then interpret these as affirming not DOA but precisely its negation. I take this to be a *reductio* of DOA as a statement that anything goes in interpreting any kind of text. In defending the thesis, I assume a narrow application to literary texts.

Another thing that is not so clear is the degree of textual openness mandated by DOA. Despite Foucault's spirit of unbridled textual freedom, he envisions some constraints in the wake of DOA, though he does not tell us what these might be.[12] For Barthes, textual meaning is a matter of reader response. Whatever serves the reader's pleasure in engaging the text is thereby justified, and here it seems anything goes, including not only multiple interpretation but avoidable contradiction and radical revision of textual data, that is, taking the words and sentences of a text, consistently or otherwise, to signify something

---

[10]DA, pp. 144-45; MA, p. 14.
[11]WIA, p. 101; QA, p. 76.
[12]WIA, p. 119; QA, p. 95.

else, a variety of things, or anything at all. In the unresigned spirit of Foucault, and quite in keeping with Barthes's view of reader response, DOA is the thesis that literary texts are interpretively open. To a certain extent, I will argue, this is not only defensible, it is perfectly compatible with disciplinary practice. It does not mean, however, that anything goes.

First Defense

Many of the arguments offered for DOA are far less persuasive than the thesis itself. In this section I criticize these arguments, most of them from ancillary theses usefully disambiguated by Peter Lamarque.[13] The first piece of support, which Lamarque calls the historicist thesis, is meant to establish that the concept AUTHOR is dispensable.[14] According to this thesis, AUTHOR is a concept that emerged only after a long history of textual production. As texts were once conceived without AUTHOR, it is not necessary to conceive of texts as authored, and so it is possible to dispense with AUTHOR.[15] Granted, a robust conception of authorial rights and responsibilities did emerge rather late in the game. Take, for example, early modern philosophers and scientists, many of whom appropriated their predecessors' ideas without what is now considered due acknowledgement or citation. In a more basic sense, however, an author is simply someone who produces a certain kind of text. Authorial rights and responsibilities are logically posterior to AUTHOR in this more basic sense, and it is far from obvious that *this* notion is a relatively new one. Even if it is, so is ELECTRON, and we can no longer dispense with ELECTRON if we are going to do physics. Perhaps, though, AUTHOR is rather more like PHLOGISTON than ELECTRON, but this suggestion, I take it, is not serious enough to merit rebuttal.

Foucault's author function thesis is meant to show not only that AUTHOR is dispensable, but that such dispensation is warranted. According to this thesis, the person designated "author" is inessential to AUTHOR, which is itself inessential to the discourses in which it func-

---

[13]Peter Lamarque, "The Death of the Author: An Analytic Autopsy," *British Journal of Aesthetics* 30 (1990): 319-31.

[14]I use capital letters to indicate the concept (e.g., "AUTHOR"), a convention used often in the philosophy of mind.

[15]DA, p. 142; MA, p. 12.

tions to delimit textual meaning.[16] Anything, a computer say, could play the same role as the designated author, because although the designate is the proximal cause of the text, AUTHOR is really that function of discourse by which, among other things, various works are clustered in the same *oeuvre*.[17] To say that x is by Shakespeare is really to say no more than x is Shakespearean, a predicate that not only clusters texts and helps delimit meaning, but eliminates reference to Shakespeare himself. Without such reference to anchor it in discourse, the predicate becomes disposable, and because it stultifies meaning rather than proliferating it, the disposal is warranted. This is Foucault's "two step." Reduce the author to a function, then dispose of the function.

Such dispensation would naturally have undesirable consequences, including by hypothesis the loss of *oeuvres* and the classificatory, explanatory, and predictive work they do. The promissory note here, implausibly, is that the benefits would outweigh the necessary harms. But the harms are hardly necessary. AUTHOR would only inhibit interpretive practice if the meaning of "author" were radically different from what it is. We can and perhaps should abandon AUTHOR if, for instance, part of the meaning of "author" is that person whose intentions determine textual meaning. But this is not part of AUTHOR.[18] If it were, anti-intentionalist hypotheses would be incoherent, for they would assert that what determines textual meaning (i.e., authorial intention) does not bear on, and hence does not determine, textual meaning. But it is not incoherent to say that the author's intentions do not determine, or are not essentially relevant to, textual meaning. By this observation alone it is not clear that we can, much less that we should, dispense with the concept AUTHOR.

Another unsuccessful attempt to undermine the author is the claim that texts do not, and cannot, express the author's creative intentions, beliefs, desires, or other mental states. The text comes into being by an act which is not expressive per se but performative, preceded by, if anything, an elliptical *I write*, the "I" being something of a formal

---

[16] WIA, pp. 118-19; QA, pp. 94-95.

[17] WIA, p. 107; QA, p. 82.

[18] Knapp and Michaels agree that the text-as-authored implies intentionalism. See Steven Knapp and Walter Benn Michaels, "Against Theory," in W.T.J. Mitchell, ed., *Against Theory: Literary Studies and the New Pragmatism* (Chicago: University of Chicago Press, 1982), p. 12. Barthes and Foucault (implausibly) deny the author in favor of a (plausible) anti-intentionalism, while Knapp and Michaels claim (plausibly) that the author is indispensable, concluding (implausibly) that intentionalism is tautologous. In both cases the suspect premise is the conditional.

indicator. This is the *écriture* thesis, according to which the act of writing does not amplify but rather silences the author's "voice" or personality.[19] This is, to say the least, a tendentious claim. Authors are not misguided in seeing the publication of their writing as ampliative in this sense, nor are critics who speak of the author's voice, or infer psychological traits of the author from the text. Although the performative view of writing is provocative, and deserves further exploration,[20] the notion that texts are not psychologically expressive is clearly untenable. Autobiographical and confessional writings are not pure fictions, after all, and even the most impersonal text provides some evidence of its progenitor's mental states. Otherwise it would be pointless to subject a patient's diary or artwork to psychological analysis. The question is not whether texts are expressive, but rather whether the psychological states expressed in and evinced by a text have any bearing on the meaning we may ascribe to it. Similar considerations apply to the notion that textual signs purporting to have real-world reference merely establish reference, if any, to other signs. If the world itself really is a text, this is exactly what we should expect reference to amount to.

One piece of support Lamarque does not discuss is the attempt to undermine authors' originality. Barthes claims that a text is "a multi-dimensional space in which a variety of writings, none of them original, blend and clash," and goes on to say that "the writer can only imitate a gesture that is always anterior, never original. His only power is to mix writings" as, as it were, a mosaicist, a syntactician, one who merely arranges prefabricated semantic items according to established syntactic rules.[21] This means that the writer is not an originator but merely a proximal cause of the text. It also means that writers cannot be credited with writing original, that is, innovative texts. Without such originary powers, authors seem uninteresting, and the privileged status afforded them by author-based criticism erodes. But this view is implausible. There are innovative texts, and it is simply irresponsible not to credit their producers accordingly. Neologism, syntactic variation, thematic novelty, and procedural departures aside, original-

---

[19]DA, p. 142; MA, p. 12.

[20]I think there is something quite provocative in the *écriture* thesis, to wit, the idea that the very act of writing is sufficient to bring a literary world into existence. If, as I hope to show, aesthetic meaning is both open and distinguishable from what it evinces of the author's psychology, then the literary text is at once expressive *and* performative, psychologically closed, aesthetically open.

[21]DA, p. 146; MA, p. 16.

ity is possible even relative to fixed vocabularies and syntax. A useful analogy here is the idea that a sufficiently long chain of deductions, each one trivial and uninformative in itself, can yield new, non-trivial knowledge, as with, for example, Gödel's proof.[22] In addition, allowing the author the sort of originality denied by Barthes in no way commits us to constraints, much less intentionalist constraints, on textual meaning. Either way, DOA is a non sequitur.

It is unfortunate that Barthes and Foucault focus so much of their attack on the author, for the author is not the only possible source of textual closure. Other candidates present themselves. In "The Intentional Fallacy," the *locus classicus* of anti-intentionalism, Wimsatt and Beardsley claim that author's meaning, a straightforward analog of speaker's meaning, is—literally "for all intents and purposes"—irrelevant to the meaning of a text.[23] Subject to the linguistic and literary conventions by which its meaning is publicly determinable, the text is not open but interpretively closed, and its meaning is that on which successively improved interpretations converge. It is odd for Barthes to claim, in this regard, that the reign of the author has coincided with the reign of the critic,[24] for if intentionalism is correct, the critic is beholden to the author, who has a significant if not indefeasible authority. But if anti-intentionalism is correct, and the text is interpretively closed, the critic stands unchallenged as *the* guru of literary significance. DOA is anathema to all such "tyrannies," authorial intention, the text itself, critical consensus, and—worst of all—readership majority. This accounts for Foucault's claim that certain notions intended to replace the author "actually seem to preserve that privilege and suppress the real meaning of his disappearance."[25]

The Presumption of Intent

The concept AUTHOR is indispensable for conceiving of and indicating the subject who, with intent, even in automatic and afflatal writing, brings the text into being. The conditions of textual emergence

---

[22]For an excellent introduction to Gödel's proof, see Ernest Nagel and James R. Newman, *Gödel's Proof* (New York: New York University Press, 1983).

[23]W.K. Wimsatt and Monroe C. Beardsley, "The Intentional Fallacy," in *The Verbal Icon: Studies in the Meaning of Poetry* (Lexington: University of Kentucky Press, 1954), pp. 3-18.

[24]DA, p. 147; MA, p. 17.

[25]WIA, p. 103; QA, p. 78.

cannot be denied or, per Barthes and Foucault, unduly diminished. While such intentions are causally relevant, what is not so clear is whether they are interpretively relevant. According to intentionalism, the meaning of a text is just what the author intended it to mean, and so interpretation ought to be accountable to what we can glean of the author's intent. Intentionalism is initially plausible, and as it implies textual closure, it is one of the views that must be undermined if DOA is to be successfully defended.

There are many reasons to reject intentionalism, not least Wimsatt's and Beardsley's classic distinction between author's meaning and textual meaning. The interpretations suggested by the author's avowed, secret, or subconscious intentions may preclude aesthetically preferable interpretations, even where these are relativized to writer-as-reader response.[26] As we know, we can interpret texts not only in ignorance but even in direct violation of the author's intentions. Dostoevsky wanted to transform Russia into a giant monastery, but his novels are better appreciated when his theological message—in Barthes's sense as well as the standard sense—is ignored. Alyosha is far less compelling than Ivan. Raskolnikov's redemption is a profound disappointment. Intentionalism is right to respect the author, but intentionalism is not the only means of doing so. We also respect authors by interpreting their work charitably, and the principle of charity requires that we not be limited to interpreting a text in accordance with the author's intentions. To be charitable to Dostoevsky, we must ignore him. One might claim that the most charitable interpretation of a text gives us access to the author's intentions, but this concedes the more important point that interpretation can proceed prior to an account of such intentions. Where a text is the only real evidence of the states of mind that produced it, as with certain anonymous texts, we can only access intentions, if we can at all, through a prior understanding of the text itself.

One might think intentionalism plausible if, for instance, one views communication as the proper function of texts. On this view, texts are designed to mediate the transmission of thoughts and feelings. Here one recalls from Prufrock "That's not what I meant. That's not what I meant at all" and imagines Eliot himself replying, "So what?" No question, the proper function of most non-literary texts is to communicate, but this is difficult to maintain for the literary text as a species

---

[26]Stephen Davies, "The Aesthetic Relevance of Authors' and Painters' Intentions," *Journal of Aesthetics and Art Criticism* 41 (1982): 65.

of artwork. *The Trial* then becomes a terribly inefficient means of conveying the idea that life is bureaucratically oppressive, implacably irrational, and irremediably bleak. One might think that what Kafka wanted to communicate requires the perlocutionary effect of *The Trial*, but why then did Kafka want the manuscript destroyed? How do we square the novel's obvious literary success with the indeterminacy of the desired communiqué? Many artists explicitly disavow the intent to communicate, and many reveal in their work things they wish they had not revealed. Surely what an artist *betrays* in art is not a matter of communication. Obscurantism and the new writing are altogether pointless if the function of art is communicative. If literary writing has any single proper function, it is, quite trivially, to create a fictional, poetic, or dramatic world. Where the purpose is to communicate, success depends on the writer's competence in the use of, or, in the case of innovation, departure from linguistic and literary conventions. But here again, reader competence in engaging the text itself is sufficient for understanding the text. A good mystery is a good mystery even if the author, on our best hypothesis, intended to write a romance. If we know a romance was intended, we might well be disappointed in the author, and although this may detract from our appreciation of the text, it need not. Even if it does, and should, this does not by itself scotch our interpreting it as a mystery.

Another challenge faced by the intentionalist is what to say about accidentally produced original texts, or, if you prefer, quasi-texts. The monkey's *Hamlet* reproduces an already authored text where at least something of the author's intentions is already known. This scenario is far less interesting than that of a dramatically great, never before inscribed *Shamlet*, accidentally produced by a monkey or a computer programmed to generate random sentences. Naturally, *Shamlet* is not a work of art. Perhaps it is not even a text, although by hypothesis it is at least a quasi-text, interpretable *as if* it were a text.[27] As far as our aesthetic interest is concerned, it might as well have been written by a playwright. By hypothesis, we can interpret *Shamlet* in full view of the fact that there is no author whose intentions we can appeal to in determining the meaning of the quasi-text. Intentionalism requires us to ignore *Shamlet*, even though it is a literary interpretable. Yet it seems we have every reason not to ignore *Shamlet*. Had it been

---

[27] I use "quasi-text" and "literary interpretable" to remain neutral on the question of whether texts must be intentionally produced. Many think not, but for an argument to the contrary see Jorge J.E. Gracia, *A Theory of Textuality: Its Logic and Epistemology* (Albany: SUNY Press, 1995), pp. 59-70.

written by a playwright, it would count not only as literature, but as great literature, eminently worthy of dramatic performance and critical attention. It is not clear why the accidental emergence of *Shamlet* should delegitimate performances of it or critical commentary on it. There is nothing wrong with finding sunsets and other natural phenomena aesthetically piquant, and so there is no reason why the aesthetic rewards of *Shamlet* should be ignored, decried, or rejected out of hand. It might be more gratifying to interpret natural phenomena as artworks in the divine *oeuvre*, and one might even appeal to such beauty in an argument from aesthetic design. The point, however, is that the piquancy of sunsets and the like does not depend on their being intentionally produced.

It is for such reasons that a cluster of views loosely affiliated with intentionalism seems more plausible than the affiliate itself. These are varieties of constructivism, according to which interpretation of a literary text requires, not prior assessment of the author's intentions, which are often unknowable, or violable, but some kind of author construct. Examples include Booth's implied author, Walton's apparent artist, Nehamas's author figure, Gracia's pseudo-historical author, and Irwin's urauthor.[28] These constructs differ in explanatory purpose and power, constraints on historical plausibility, and degree of affiliation with intentionalism. What they share is the view that, without an author construct, interpretation is hamstrung. Ignorance or violation of the author's intentions is thus compatible, at least potentially, with textual closure via an author construct. Robert Stecker argues that such constructs are reducible to hypotheses about what the real author intended, in which case constructivism is on the same footing as intentionalism.[29] While Stecker's argument is persuasive, we might well construct a Dostoevsky whose message accords, not with the message of the man himself, but with our best, most charitable interpretation of his novels. Furthermore, it seems we can and perhaps should construct an author for *Shamlet*, in which case author constructs are not,

---

[28]Wayne C. Booth, *The Rhetoric of Fiction* (Chicago: University of Chicago Press, 1961), p. 73; Kendal Walton, "Style and the Products and Processes of Art," in Berel Lang, ed., *The Concept of Style* (Philadelphia: University of Pennsylvania Press, 1979), p. 53; Alexander Nehamas, "Writer, Text, Work, Author," in A.J. Cascardi, ed., *Literature and the Question of Philosophy* (Baltimore: Johns Hopkins University Press, 1987), p. 285; Gracia, *Theory of Textuality*, p. 4; William Irwin, *Intentionalist Interpretation: A Philosophical Explanation and Defense* (Westport: Greenwood Press, 1999), p. 30.

[29]Robert Stecker, "Apparent, Implied, and Postulated Authors," *Philosophy and Literature* 11 (1987): 258-71.

generally speaking, reducible to hypotheses about what the real author intended. Constructivism thus has the relative advantage over intentionalism in allowing interpretation in ignorance or in violation of intended meaning, and of quasi-texts which merit literary attention.

What the *Shamlet* case shows, however, is that interpretation requires a *presumption of intent*, in that literary interpretables are taken to issue from, or as though from, intentions. Unlike interest in sunsets and other natural phenomena, our interest in *Shamlet* is asymmetrically dependent on our interest in written art, which, although produced under the auspices of bona fide intent, is interpretable irrespective of such intentional *content* as we may discover or ascribe. If we discovered that *Hamlet* really is a kind of *Shamlet*, this would undermine the belief that it is a work of art, not the belief that it is a literary interpretable. But the quasi-text is a literary interpretable in virtue of certain resemblances between it and genuine texts. Can we build an author construct for *Shamlet*? Of course. Must we? It seems not, given our knowledge of the accidental emergence of the quasi-text. If we must, our only means of doing so is by inference from what we can glean from *Shamlet*. But this means we derive the construct from the interpretation, not the other way around. What remains is a more or less empty constructivism. The one inescapable feature of the author construct, it seems, is that the text be treated as though it is an intentional artifact. This does not vindicate constructivism, however, for the requirement that a literary interpretable be taken as though intended does not mean that the content of such intent has any bearing on textual meaning. Without purchase on textual meaning, the presumption of intent yields an *abstractum* too minimal to count as a genuine author construct. Nonetheless, it is in this presumption that the marginal life of the author consists.

Intentionalism and constructivism are tempting because accessing the author's real or constructed intentions gives us an explanatory advantage vis-à-vis the text. Authorial vision, in other words, provides a top-down means to interpret textual data. But for reasons that should now be clear, this advantage may be illusory, unduly limiting, or superfluous. Robust author constructs are consequently dispensable. We do not need such a construct (i.e., God) to interpret the world, so why should we need one to interpret a literary world? Indeed, God-based worldviews, at least historically, have had the unduly limiting or superfluous role attributable to author-based and constructivist criticism. This is not to say that the DOA case has been won, or that traditional interpretive and critical practice is illegitimate *tout court*. It is rather to say that, at this point, DOA is defensible from two potential sources of textual closure.

Aesthetic Meaning

According to Barthes, "a text's unity lies not in its origin but in its destination."[30] But as we have seen, we need not deny the author's antecedent creative vision to allow for liberation from authorial intention. Colin Lyas writes: "The alternative seems merely to replace authorial will with audience whim."[31] Short of reader response, however, we are now left with the text itself, subject to linguistic and literary conventions to which innovation is tractable as a departure. The text may provide its own interpretive closure, or rather convention might close it for us. The most difficult hurdle for advocates of DOA is not intentionalism and constructivism after all. It is rather the text itself, for textual data seem unrevisable, fixing meaning locally and determining the *gestalt*. Beyond mere underdetermination, indeterminacy in a literary world can be seen as an unimportant consequence of the fact that finite texts are incomplete. The meaning of a literary text might be said to consist in unrevisable textual data and such further determinable, though underdetermined, meaning as can be inferred from them.

The question now is how an advocate of DOA can dispose of the text itself as interpretively closed. One move is to grant that intentions do determine textual meaning while insisting that authorial intention is interpretively open. If the text is our best and sometimes only evidence of authorial intention, and evinces an indefinite disjunction of plausible intentions, then it is interpretively open. There are other kinds of evidence besides the text, however. These include biographical, historical, and psychological evidence, and in many cases these are usefully available for paring down the disjunction. Suppose that, from the initial conception of a text to its final execution, we know all there is to know about the author's brain. We might maintain that to build a profile of the author's intentions from this neurological knowledge is, at best, to engage in radical translation, where there is no canoni-

---

[30]DA, p. 148; MA, p. 17.
[31]Colin Lyas, "Intention," in D.E. Cooper, ed., *A Companion to Aesthetics* (Oxford: Blackwell, 1996), p. 230.

cal interpretation, no fact of the matter about the mental content we seek to discover. We might even say that all interpretation amounts to radical translation. Either way, the text will be interpretively open.

But suppose the advocate of DOA is quite rightly unpersuaded that radical translation is endemic either to a general theory of meaning or to the determination of an author's intentions. In other words, suppose the advocate rejects meaning holism in general and accepts psychological realism in particular. Certainly DOA would be far less interesting as a mere consequence of an otherwise unrelated theory of meaning. What is the DOA advocate to do? First, admit that the author's intentions and the text issuing from them are interpretively closed vis-à-vis the author's neuropsychology. Second, admit also that, relative to certain interpretive methods and purposes, literary conventions may tightly circumscribe textual meaning. Third, insist that none of this bears on textual meaning in the relevant sense, that of limiting how a reader may interpret a text. If nothing else, reader's meaning is, in principle at least, no less legitimate than writer's meaning, and it is after all in the *reading* of texts that multiple interpretability is fully appreciable. Various conventions may delimit acceptable interpretations, but readers concerned only with maximizing their own aesthetic experience have no other reason to bother with them, much less sacrifice their interpretations to those that are conventionally preferred. Relegating the sources of closure to other domains, the advocate has both the room, and the obligation, to formulate an account of such meaning as allows for the interpretive openness of literary texts.

As distinct from both intended and conventional meaning, the aesthetic meaning of a text can be understood in terms of those interpretations which variously and idiosyncratically facilitate the reader's appreciation, particularly what I elsewhere call *resolutive* experience—mutually coherent intellectual and emotional responses.[32] Piquant interpretations will vary from one person to another, and the more the individual reader allows meaning to proliferate, the more profound the resolutive experience. This latter claim is, within limits, psychologically plausible. The more meanings, or layers of meaning, are read into a text, the more one tends to appreciate it. In this way, aesthetic meaning is pluralistic, as DOA requires, both across individuals and, at least as a matter of psychological tendency, within individuals. I write "at least as a matter of tendency" because, in the name of reader

---

[32] Jason Holt, "A Comprehensivist Theory of Art," *British Journal of Aesthetics* 36 (1996): 427.

liberation, it seems one cannot rule out either the possibility or the legitimacy of someone finding unisemous interpretation aesthetically optimal. Some have a need to simplify literary texts, finding them less pleasing otherwise. While this may betray a lack of refinement, neither Barthes nor Foucault can consistently rule it out of what the liberated reader may do.

Disciplinary Practice and Reader Response

The upshot of all this might seem to be that in interpreting literary texts, anything goes, and disciplinary practice is consequently groundless. If DOA implied this, it would not be defensible. But reader liberation does seem to imply that I may interpret a literary text any way I wish. I can stipulate, for instance, that *Ulysses* means "the cat is on the mat," or something equally absurd. In what ways might such a stipulation be defeasible? Stipulations are arbitrary assignments of meaning, and there is nothing wrong with them in principle. They have their uses, and that, indeed, is the point. Stipulation is purposive, and so is evaluable relative to the achievement and the value of such purposes. Stipulating that simulacra of the *Mona Lisa* will stand for some predicate in quantificational logic is pragmatically defeasible, as would be, in all likelihood, the *Ulysses* stipulation. The *Ulysses* stipulation might also be dismissed if it is put to an illicit purpose, to undermine the work by unfair means, to deceive a gullible audience, to interfere with fruitful discussion, and so on. In such cases, it is unclear that the stipulation would even count as an interpretation. So the *Ulysses* stipulation is potentially dismissible on a number of grounds. Although such grounds are extra-literary, they are sufficient to undermine idiosyncratic stipulations that are not in service of the stipulator's aesthetic appreciation.

In service of their own aesthetic experience, however, readers are free to interpret literary texts any way they want. Suppose, for instance, that someone finds the *Ulysses* stipulation piquant. We may dismiss the case as psychologically aberrant, and we may deny, for this reason, that the interpretation is likely to foster others' appreciation. At the same time, we have no legitimate grounds to deny readers what serves their legitimate aesthetic interest. In what sense then is there room for disciplinary practice? Plenty. Disciplinary practice needs criteria for better and worse interpretations, and nothing

41

here prevents individuals from getting together and agreeing on the methods by which and the purposes for which they will proceed to interpret texts. Aesthetic interest may be provisionally sacrificed, by mutual agreement, for the investigation of the text-as-world, where such understanding is an end in itself or a means to augmenting deferred appreciation. Here, by default, the text loses some but not all of its plasticity as an erstwhile open interpretable, because the justification of interpretations will be constrained by intersubjective methods and purposes. With standards and purposes set, interpretations will be evaluable relative to those standards and purposes, and *gestalt* interpretations will ideally be successively improved in reflective equilibrium with low-level interpretations of textual data.

As different sets of readers can adopt different standards and purposes, there is plenty of room for disciplinary pluralism in an institutional context. This is a *desideratum* if one looks without a completely jaundiced eye at the present state of the art. However, just as in the case of the lone reader's stipulations, a subdiscipline can be evaluated relative to the achievement and the value of its purposes. On extraliterary grounds, some research programs simply will not cut it. But even within a legitimate subdiscipline, there is no reason to expect textual closure. From the perspective of Marxist criticism, is *Atlas Shrugged* a symptom of the medial stage of the dialectic, a *reductio* of nonmaterialist or nondeterminist views, propaganda, or dystopia? What various interpretations fit *Atlas Shrugged* from a feminist perspective? Is *Don Quixote* a satire or a celebration of self-ennoblement? Should textual ambiguities, like Othello's famous "Let it alone," be resolved as a matter of fact? Is there any textual datum so fixed that it is not in principle revisable? Procedures can always be developed to close a text, but the closure will be artificial, and may yield inferior interpretations when applied to other texts.

On a related tack, there is nothing wrong with critics directing the reader's attention to good texts and to potentially piquant interpretations or interpretive procedures. Nor is there anything wrong with investigating the author in a psychology, history, or mechanics of the literary process, so long as what we discover of the author's vision, circumstances, or technique does not impede the pursuit of better textual interpretations. Assessing the extent to which a text realizes its author's vision requires this mutual independence. As meaning should proliferate within certain limits, so should disciplinary practice. To rule out disciplinary practice altogether, as Barthes and Foucault seem to imply, or to insist on one method or purpose as canonical, is not, after all, in the spirit or to the purpose of reader liberation. This is an important point to emphasize. DOA is in fact compatible with a virtuous mean between nihilism and dogmatism in disciplinary practice.

Although DOA is largely defensible, it is not so in virtue of the major arguments adduced by Barthes and Foucault. While literary texts are interpretively open, this does not mean that, in interpretive matters, anything goes. There are constraints on what counts as a viable interpretation, even for liberated readers in the privacy of their thoughts, for not just any interpretation will facilitate a reader's aesthetic appreciation, and those that do will, as a matter of human psychology, if not logical consistency, exclude many others. This is owing to the limits of attention and the relative implasticity of an individual's taste. But it is for a more important reason that the "D" in DOA turns out to be slightly inapt. What we cannot escape in interpreting a literary text or quasi-text is what I have called the presumption of intent, by which any literary interpretable is taken as, or as though, the product of intentions, the content of which, however, need not concern us. It is in this presumption, I have argued, that the marginal life of the author consists, leaving the author as good as dead, but not dead in fact, and leaving thanatophiles, aptly enough, with a polysemous challenge, to wit, and simply, *habeas corpus*.[33]

[33]For helpful comments I thank William Irwin, Deborah Knight, and Rhonda Martens. For useful discussion I thank Elana Geller, Larry Holt, Carl Matheson, and Adam Muller.

4 Ex Ante Allusions

We tend to think of allusions as indirect references to objects that already exist. Here I challenge this post facto orthodoxy, and propose an alternative account of literary allusion not as reference to but as reference from. In particular, I argue that the notion of ex ante allusion—literally 'from before,' i.e. to objects that do not yet exist—is perfectly coherent despite its paradoxical veneer, that there are actual examples of such allusions in select literary works, and that although these examples are generally hard to verify, the fact that they do exist suggests important revisions to our concept of allusion.

To begin, take the definition proposed by William Irwin in his important philosophical analysis, 'What Is an Allusion?': Irwin defines allusion as 'a reference that is indirect in the sense that it calls for associations that go beyond mere substitution of a referent'[1]—we might compress this for now into 'reference by association.' What Irwin intends here is twofold: first, to distinguish allusion from other sorts of reference, typically more direct references; second, to identify the psychological mechanism (i.e. association) that makes it work and that characterizes its special indirectness. To take an example, in Leonard Cohen's poem 'Thousand Kisses Deep,' the lines 'And maybe I had miles to drive / *And promises to keep*' rather clearly allude to Robert Frost's 'Stopping by Woods on a Snowy Evening,' in particular the lines 'But I have promises to keep, / And miles to go before I sleep...'[2] By contrast, and taking Irwin's definition strictly, the phrase 'the gloomy Dane,' though certainly a reference to Hamlet, is too direct (as it constitutes 'mere substitution of a referent') to be an allusion to Hamlet, though perhaps not too direct to be used to allude

---

[1] Irwin 2001, 289.
[2] Cohen 2006, 57; Frost 1940, 310.

to *Hamlet*.

For a discussion case, Irwin offers 'I am not Prufrock' as a candidate allusion, though not to the character in Eliot's poem 'The Love Song of J. Alfred Prufrock.' It is an allusion rather to some facet(s) of the subject that we are meant to associate with the Prufrock character in the poem—whatever that might be, perhaps that the subject does not consider himself as insignificant or as life having passed him by.[3] This is clearly a literary reference, and we even sometimes speak of such references as literary allusions even though the literary referent is not identical to the object of the allusion. We may sympathize with the complaint that such a literary reference is too direct to constitute a literary allusion insofar as it is not itself referred to by association; rather, it is the literary basis of the allusion to something else, and in this sense we should distinguish two types of literary allusion: allusion to a literary work (as with Cohen's allusion to Frost) versus allusion through a literary work (as with the Prufrock example). I suggest that we designate these 'type 1' and 'type 2' literary allusions, respectively. Although allusions can occur outside the confines of literature and art generally—allusions that have nothing to do with art; neither in, nor about, nor that use it at all—it is artistic, and chiefly literary, allusions that concern me here.

To understand the associative link between allusions and their objects it will be helpful to revisit Hume's distinction among principles of association. The *Treatise* famously distinguishes among three principles by which ideas suggest one another: resemblance, contiguity, and causation.[4] It is by resembling the person that a portrait tends to make one think of the person. Likewise, it is by the resemblance between Cohen's 'miles to drive... promises to keep' and Frost's 'promises to keep... miles to go' that Cohen alludes to Frost. Turning to contiguity, thinking about Canada may bring to mind its neighbour to the south, the United States. In same way, at a presentation characterized by unusual levels of bombast and platitude, I might whisper to a colleague 'So he advises Laertes,' thus alluding to Polonius, a contiguous character in the same play. In this way too we can allude to a work by quoting it, in that the quotation is contiguous with the other parts that together constitute the whole. Although it may not be immediately apparent, the principle of causation also figures into

---

[3]Irwin 2001, 287. The particular context often enough will help disambiguate the meaning of this or any other type of allusion.

[4]See Hume 1926, 1.1.4.1-5, 19-21.

allusion. In typical cases, the object of allusion inspires, and so is part of the causal story behind, the allusion itself. More important for my purposes, if I am correct in my claim that there is such a thing as ex ante allusion, the associative principle of causation will help explain how such allusions work.

I

Before arguing that the notion of ex ante allusions is coherent, however, it makes sense first to outline what I call the post facto orthodoxy, which is part of the standard view of allusions that, both pre-critically and theoretically, sometimes explicitly and sometimes implicitly, denies the very possibility of ex ante allusions.

Consider first various characterizations of allusion in prominent literary reference books. *A New Handbook of Literary Terms*: 'When a literary work engages in allusion, it refers to—plays with, makes use of—*earlier* pieces of literature (or, sometimes, history)' (emphasis added).[5] *The New Princeton Encyclopedia of Poetry and Poetics* defines allusion as the 'deliberate incorporation of identifiable elements from other sources, *preceding or contemporaneous*, textual or extratextual' (emphasis added).[6] Even when such a restriction is not explicitly put on allusion, it is usually, if less obviously, present in the form of an implication; for instance, take the definition of allusion from the *Oxford Dictionary of Literary Terms*:

> An indirect or passing reference to some event, person, place, or artistic work, the nature and relevance of which is not explained by the writer but *relies on the reader's familiarity* with what is thus mentioned (emphasis added).[7]

Although there is no explicit requirement here that the object of allusion already exist, this does seem to be implied by the stress placed on reader familiarity, for a reader cannot be familiar with a text or something else that does not yet exist. This is what I mean by the phrase 'the post facto orthodoxy,' which amounts to ruling out the possibility of ex ante allusions, since these different characterizations of allusion

---

[5]Mikics 2010, 11.
[6]Preminger and Brogan 1993, 38-39.
[7]Baldrick 2009, 9.

are intended to express not just what is typical of such reference but what is essential to it.

The post facto orthodoxy is not merely part of the establishment view of allusion as expressed in literary reference books. It is a commitment shared by many philosophers as well. Consider first the conceptual analysis proposed by Göran Hermerén, which amounts to the following necessary and sufficient conditions. According to Hermerén, an allusion has occurred if an only if:

> (1) The artist intended to make beholders think of the *earlier* work by giving his work certain features. (2) As a matter of fact beholders contemplating his work make associations with that *earlier* work. (3) These beholders recognize that this is what the artist (among other things) intended to achieve (emphasis added).[8]

Leaving aside the fact that some objects of allusion are not works of art, this is a clear, explicit commitment to the post facto orthodoxy. We likewise see such a commitment in the explication of allusion (specifically in film) offered by Noël Carroll:

> Allusion, as I am using it, is an umbrella term covering a mixed lot of practices including *quotations*, the memorialization of *past* genres, the *reworking* of past genres, *homages*, and the *recreation* of "classic" scenes, shots, plot motifs, lines of dialogue, themes, gestures, and so forth from film *history* (emphasis added).[9]

As above, even when it is not explicitly part of a definition of allusion, the post facto orthodoxy tends to reveal itself in the interpretation of the definition's scope. For instance, although Irwin's definition of allusion as reference by association does not obviously rule out ex ante allusions, in developing his account Irwin makes perfectly clear that he embraces the restriction. As he puts it, 'Only a divine author, outside of time, would seem capable of alluding to a later text.'[10]

Irwin makes this claim as if it were not expected to be in any way controversial. Indeed, it is not particularly controversial, which reflects the fact that the post facto orthodoxy is often taken for granted, and

---

[8] Hermerén 1992, 211.
[9] Carroll 1998, 241.
[10] Irwin 2001, 297 n22.

so constitutes an important yet, I argue, challengeable part of the conventional view of allusions.

II

Let us turn now to three candidate cases for the label 'ex ante allusion,' which I have chosen for various reasons. The first two cases are intended to demonstrate the coherence of the concept, to stand as possible cases of ex ante allusion. The third case, though rather obscure by contrast with the first two, is intended to stand not merely as a possible instance but as a confirmed actual case.

The first case comes from Ernest Hemingway and *The Sun Also Rises*. The book's protagonist is Jake Barnes, and the novel is written in the first person from Jake's perspective. There is reason to interpret Jake as Hemingway's fictional stand-in, including the common interpretation of the novel as a roman à clef. Early on in the novel, another character, Robert Cohn, in the context of what can only be described as an existential conversation, asks Jake, 'Do you know that in about thirty-five years more we'll be dead?'[11] Note that: thirty-five years; and note that the novel was originally copyrighted and first published in 1926. Add 35 to 1926, and you get 1961; and 1961 was the very year Hemingway committed suicide![12] At the very least, the juxtaposition of such a fictional prediction with covert real-world implications, apparently fulfilled many decades after the fact, is apt to give one pause.

To be absolutely clear here, my claim is not that this necessarily *is* a case of ex ante allusion. My claim is only that it *might* be. It is at least possible that Hemingway had the intention, in 1926, to commit suicide thirty-five years later, and that he also had an intention to allude, covertly, to this eventuality by putting the prediction in the mouth of a fictional character addressing, in fictional disguise, Hemingway himself. I admit, openly, that this case is likely just a coincidence, that the timing of the suicide was not deliberate or, if it was, had nothing to do with the novel's apparent if merely possible prediction. Well and good. The point remains, however: although this was, in all probability, mere coincidence, it might not have been. The suicide might have fulfilled an ex ante allusion, and if so, what an astonishing

---

[11]Hemingway 1954, 11.

[12]This observation was originally made and discussed in Holt 2013.

moment in literary history!—Hemingway coming to fulfil the prophecy of his first great work, and thereby enhancing its greatness, with a unique and profound, ultimately the grandest, gesture.

The second case comes from Leonard Cohen, and is similar to the first insofar as it is intended to demonstrate the coherence of the concept of ex ante allusion without serving as a verifiable case, at least given the information now available to us. Whereas Hemingway is dead, Cohen is, at the time of writing this essay, still living, and so unlike Hemingway might provide evidence that his case counts, or fails to, as ex ante allusion. The case is as follows: in his 2001 song 'That Don't Make It Junk,' Leonard Cohen speaks of having closed, as he calls it, the Book of Longing. This could well have been an ex ante allusion to his poetry collection published five years later, *Book of Longing*.[13] That is, Cohen could have written the line about closing the Book of Longing with the intention of alluding to an envisioned but not then existing work. I am not suggesting that an intention to allude is sufficient for an allusion to have occurred, but rather only that such intent is a key ingredient of and so good evidence for allusion.[14]

There are two reasons why this might not count as an ex ante allusion. First, Cohen might have written the line and only *later* come to consider that it would make a good title. In this case the possible ex ante allusion may simply reduce to typical self-influence. Second, it might seem too direct a reference to count as an allusion proper. Although the first concern cannot be answered at this point, something may be said to the second. Although it seems 'the Book of Longing' is a rather direct reference to *Book of Longing*, it is rather perhaps more indirect than it appears. The original phrase includes the definite article, lacks italics, and in context is better interpreted not as a book in its own right but as either a metaphorical book or an imagined biblical book. In any event, if this reference is too direct, it might have been made less directly. So again, even if we cannot say for sure that this is an actual case of ex ante allusion—that it may amount to no more than post facto influence, that it might be too direct—it could have been otherwise and so further illustrates the possibility of such.

The third case is an obscure one but, in a way, more to the point, illustrating, I claim, not merely the coherence of the concept, but an actual case of ex ante allusion. An experimental novel was published

---

[13] Cohen 2006.

[14] For instance, an attempt to allude via quotation can go awry if the quotation is misattributed or the correct source is unrecognizably misquoted.

in 2003 by a relatively unknown writer named Jason Holt, bearing the title *The Black Books Addiction*. Nothing in the novel itself suggests the title, except for the paperback's cover, which is self-referentially black. Any expectation of exploring the suggested theme of literature-as-narcotic is disappointed by the novel itself, although ultimately fulfilled by the author's 2009 follow-up, *A Tangent at 3:15*, which takes literature-as-narcotic as its key plot point. Unlike the Hemingway and Cohen cases, where we as yet lack information that would confirm or confute an ex ante hypothesis, in this case the author has confirmed the intention, when writing the 2003 book, to allude to the then-unwritten one.[15] The presence of such an intention allows us to rule out the confuting possibilities remaining live in the Hemingway and Cohen cases. This obscure novelist has, it seems, provided us with a verified case of ex ante allusion.

III

In discussing ex ante allusions and their implications I want to explain both why they have such a paradoxical veneer and why it is only that, a veneer. I also want to sketch a view, suggested by this discussion, of literary allusions as reference *from* rather than reference *to*.

First, at least part of what makes ex ante allusions seem para-doxical is a failure to appreciate the distinction between the object of allusion being *extant* and the object of allusion being *known*. In typical allusions, the object is known in virtue of, among other things, existing already. Cohen's allusion to 'Stopping by Woods on a Snowy Evening,' for instance, depends on his knowing that poem, which is knowledge he would not have if the poem did not exist. This is not because such knowledge depends on the poem already existing, but because, given Frost's authorship, Cohen was not in a position to have such knowledge until the poem had already been written. However, this is decidedly *not* the case for Cohen's epistemic access to his own envisioned but unexecuted works—e.g. the possible ex ante allusion to *Book of Longing*. This is obviously a special kind of knowledge, the knowledge on which ex ante allusions depend, as the same per-son is responsible, as alluder, both for the allusion itself as a kind of prediction, and for fulfilling the prediction by bringing the object into existence later on. Whether this counts as knowledge by description

---

[15] Personal communication.

or a special kind of knowledge by acquaintance—through the vision that inspires and shapes the later object's creation—such knowledge, though special, is indeed possible.

Skepticism about ex ante allusions could be motivated by the fact that very often we might not be able to tell whether we have an ex ante allusion rather than an instance of the far more common phenomenon of post facto influence. But this does not alter the fact that there *is* a real difference between these ex ante and post facto scenarios, a difference both causal and psychological, even if we are rarely able to sift the ex ante from the post facto. Even if Cohen never reveals it—and artists, we know, are often coy about such things—there is a fact of the matter about whether he had alluded ex ante to *Book of Longing*. Skeptics may also note that in the end ex ante allusions amount to a special and interesting form of foreshadowing, and no one doubts existence of such a common artistic device. Of course the key difference between common foreshadowing and ex ante allusions is that typical foreshadowing is of later elements in the *same* work, where ex ante allusions take objects that are decidedly extrinsic to the work. Other interwork connectors, such as cliffhangers, will often seem less like ex ante allusions and more like formal placeholders for future filling in.[16]

The paradoxical veneer of ex ante allusions owes in no small part, I suggest, to their *promissory* nature. Indeed, an intended ex ante allusion may not come off because its envisioned object does not, for whatever reason, come into being. There is, in other words, a kind of fragile contingency unique among allusions of the ex ante variety. That such an allusion may not come off, however, does not mean that when it does come off, it is not what it was intended to be. There are various respects in which ex ante allusions exhibit such a promissory character. First, until their objects eventuate, and whatever the author's intentions, there will be no shared reference with readers—although one of the lessons of modernism seems to be that the opacity of an allusion is no mark against its status as such. Ex ante allusions are also promissory in that they are arguably part of works that remain, until their objects eventuate, incomplete. They are *finished* works, to be sure, as they need no more work to be done on them, yet still lack-

---

[16]Similarly, we may also distinguish the type of open-ended, future-directed reference discussed by Hirsch 1994, 552-553. Instead of allowing for future particulars that are as yet unknown, ex ante allusions require prior knowledge of particulars not yet extant.

ing some of their raw material, they are not yet complete.[17] Third, ex ante allusions also have an element of self-fulfilling prophecy, and until fulfilled they remain allusions in progress.[18] This is why they suggest Hume's view of causation qua principle of association of ideas. The reference-by-association of an allusion can be achieved ex ante when it itself is productive of, or deliberately part of the causal fabric that ends up producing, its eventual object. An ex ante allusion is its object's causal precursor. Once the elusive object has been realized, readers may associate it with its allusive precursor whether or not they can discern its ex ante status.

If ex ante allusions do belong in the taxonomy of allusions alongside more garden variety sorts, they help motivate changes to our concept of allusion beyond such inclusion, or in other words, beyond mere rejection of the post facto orthodoxy. To return to our earlier examples, we might reconsider whether typical literary allusions, be they type 1 (Cohen alluding to Frost) or type 2 (alluding through Prufrock), as references by association, are actually references *to* literature at all. Suppose we try to account for such reference in terms of a somewhat naïve Fregean story in terms of which Cohen's use of 'miles to drive... promises to keep' alludes to Frost's 'promises to keep... miles to go' in virtue of expressing a sense that determines such reference. Well and good, except for that fact that (1) this neither accounts for the associative mechanism of allusion nor differentiates it from typical reference; (2) it therefore neglects the typical point of allusions, which is subsidiary, often ornamental, as far as their main reference is concerned—in the Cohen case, certain possibilities ('And maybe I...'), in the Prufrock case, an unidentified subject ('I am not...'); (3) it also therefore fails to respect ex ante allusions' veneer of paradoxicality, since it is not even seemingly paradoxical to simply refer, in the usual way, to something in the future.

To account for the allusive part of such references, and their subsidiary, associative, mediating role, and to respect the apparent paradoxical nature of ex ante allusions, I propose that we recast literary allusion as reference *from* rather than reference *to*, in that the main reference is achieved in such cases *via* the literary object: allusion to

---

[17]Objects of allusion may be thought of as raw materials just as clay is to sculpture. The *Venus de Milo* counts as a finished but, because of its missing pieces, incomplete work.

[18]Typical prophecies, by contrast, are more direct references, their main purpose is to proclaim rather than hint at future events, and they are uninvolved in producing what they predict.

as reference from. In type 1 cases, like the Cohen example, reference to the literary object (e.g. certain possibilities) is *from* the allusive object (e.g. Frost). Type 2 cases, conversely, exhibit reference *from* the literary object (e.g. Prufrock) to the allusive object (e.g. the unidentified subject). Here we also respect the paradoxical veneer of ex ante allusions: 'the Book of Longing' (perhaps) referring from the later *Book of Longing* to the then-current metaphor, 'thirty-five years more' (perhaps) referring from Hemingway's eventual suicide to *The Sun Also Rises'* fictional future, 'the black books addiction' (definitely) referring from the later book (as plot point) to the earlier one (as title). Thus allusion to as reference from makes sense of such references as a type of framing device.

Having argued for ex ante allusions both as a coherent possibility and a plausible actuality, and after exploring briefly some of the implications of this position, including an account of literary allusion as reference from, I conclude by acknowledging skepticism about whether this account of can be generalized to account for all allusions. This skepticism owes quite simply to the fact that some allusions no doubt are made for their own sake alone, and need not serve, beyond the pale of art, some other referential or ornamental objective.[19]

References

Baldrick, Chris. 2009. *Oxford Dictionary of Literary Terms*. Oxford: Oxford University Press.

Carroll, Noël. 1998. *Interpreting the Moving Image*. Cambridge: Cambridge University Press.

Cohen, Leonard. 2006. *Book of Longing*. Toronto: McClelland & Stewart.

Frost, Robert. 1940. "Stopping by Woods on a Snowy Evening." In *The Pocket Book of Verse*, edited by M.E. Speare, 309-310. New York: Pocket Books.

Hemingway, Ernest. 1954. *The Sun Also Rises*. New York: Charles Scribner's Sons.

---

[19]I would like to thank an anonymous reviewer for helpful comments. An earlier version of this article was presented at the 2014 meeting of the Atlantic Region Philosophers' Association.

Hermerén, Göran. 1992. "Allusions and Intentions." In *Intention and Interpretation*, edited by Gary Iseminger, 203-220. Philadelphia: Temple University Press.

Hirsch, E.D. 1994. "Transhistorical Intentions and the Persistence of Allegory," *New Literary History* 25: 549-567.

Holt, Jason. 2013. "Hemingway's Death in *The Sun Also Rises.*" *Pennsylvania Literary Journal* 5: 37-40.

Hume, David. 1926. *A Treatise of Human Nature.* London: J.M. Dent.

Irwin, William. 2001. "What Is an Allusion?" *Journal of Aesthetics and Art Criticis*m 59: 287-297.

Mikics, David. 2010. *A New Handbook of Literary Terms.* New Haven: Yale University Press.

Preminger, Alex, and T.V.F. Brogan, eds. 1993. *The New Princeton Dictionary of Poetry and Poetics.* Princeton: Princeton University Press.

5 PROVIDING FOR AESTHETIC EXPERIENCE

1. Introduction

Aesthetic theories of art are those that tie art essentially to the aesthetic, typically by way of a necessary condition that makes reference to an aesthetically qualified kind (aesthetic experience, properties, objects, purposes, interest, value, and so on).[1] Such theories hold that a thing must meet the aesthetic condition in order to count as art. In this article, I will understand the aesthetic condition in terms of aesthetic experience, as other formulations can be paraphrased in such terms and objections to aesthetic theories stand out in starkest relief from them. By the phrase "aesthetic experience" I mean nominally the distinctively pleasurable, meaningful, and valuable type of experience associated closely, though not exclusively, with the appreciation of artworks. (For now this designation should suffice, although I will provide a more detailed account below.)

---

[1] Examples include George Schlesinger, "Aesthetic Experience and the Definition of Art," *British Journal of Aesthetics* 19 (1979), pp. 167-76; Monroe C. Beardsley, "An Aesthetic Definition of Art," in *What Is Art?* ed. Hugh Curtler (New York: Haven, 1983), pp. 15-29; William Tolhurst, "Toward an Aesthetic Account of the Nature of Art," *Journal of Aesthetics and Art Criticism* 42 (1984), pp. 261-69; P.N. Humble, "The Philosophical Challenge of Avant-garde Art," *British Journal of Aesthetics* 24 (1984), pp. 119-28; Richard Lind, "The Aesthetic Essence of Art," *Journal of Aesthetics and Art Criticism* 50 (1992), pp. 117-29; James Anderson, "Aesthetic Concepts of Art," in *Theories of Art Today*, ed. Noël Carroll (Madison, WI: University of Wisconsin Press, 2000), pp. 65-92; and Nick Zangwill, "Aesthetic Functionalism," in *Aesthetic Concepts: Essays After Sibley*, eds. Emily Brady and Jerrold Levinson (Oxford: Oxford University Press, 2001), pp. 123-48.

We often think of artworks as having the function, at least typically, of providing for aesthetic experience; they yield or are meant to yield experiences of this characteristic type. We speak of art causing, or eliciting, such experiences in an appropriately situated viewer, who has the wherewithal (attentiveness, understanding, responsiveness) to be so moved. As such, aesthetic theories reflect a common and intuitive view of what artworks are and how they function.

Against this view that art can be defined, even in part, aesthetically, critics have levied several key objections (the anti-art objection, the circularity objection, the bad-art objection, the many-roles objection, and the denied-aesthetic objection). It is because of these objections that, despite recent attempts to revive it,[2] the aesthetic approach remains largely in disrepute. An aesthetic theory of art, to prove successful, must answer these objections. My purpose is to do just that, by first proposing an aesthetic criterion for art and then defending it from these objections.

2. Two Types of Aesthetic Theory

In considering aesthetic theories of art, there is a crucial distinction which not only critics but also advocates often fail to appreciate sufficiently. An aesthetic theory might require, on the one hand, that artworks *actually* provide for aesthetic experience, and on the other, that they merely be *intended* so to provide. Consider the following definitions of art (*sans definiendum*), proposed by George Schlesinger and Monroe Beardsley, respectively: "an artifact which under standard conditions *provides* its percipient with aesthetic experience"[3] (my emphasis); "something produced with the *intention* of giving it the capacity to satisfy aesthetic interest"[4] (my emphasis). We might refer to these different commitments as aesthetic *actualism* and aesthetic *intentionalism*, respectively.[5]

---

[2]See, e.g., Richard Shusterman, "The End of Aesthetic Experience," *Journal of Aesthetics and Art Criticism* 55 (1997), pp. 29-41; Anderson, "Aesthetic Concepts of Art"; Nick Zangwill, "Are There Counterexamples to Aesthetic Theories of Art?" *Journal of Aesthetics and Art Criticism* 60 (2002), pp. 111-18; and Gary Iseminger, *The Aesthetic Function of Art* (Ithaca, NY: Cornell University Press, 2004).

[3]Schlesinger, "Aesthetic Experience and the Definition of Art," p. 175.

[4]Beardsley, "An Aesthetic Definition of Art," p. 19.

[5]For discussion along somewhat different lines, see Anderson, "Aesthetic Concepts of Art." Zangwill, in "Aesthetic Functionalism," offers a more or less hybrid

Both definitions are held by critics as examples of the *same* species of aesthetic (sometimes "functionalist") theory, and criticized on that basis,[6] even though accounts like Schlesinger's are radically different from those like Beardsley's. The difference is clear and crucial. An unintentionally effective work counts as art on Schlesinger's view but not on Beardsley's. Likewise, a really poor artwork may fail to provide for aesthetic experience despite intentions to the contrary, which would qualify it as art on Beardsley's view, but not on Schlesinger's. Critics of aesthetic theories often aim their objections—each counting far more persuasively against one than against the other type of theory—indiscriminately at both, thus equivocating on what aesthetic theories imply.

Before offering a specific aesthetic criterion to defend against the key objections to aesthetic theories generally, one added refinement is in order. Critics often overextend the intended scope of aesthetic conditions, whether actualist or intentionalist, beyond the pale of plausibility. Note that no artwork causes aesthetic experience for everybody or at all times; the greatest artwork leaves some critics cold (A. C. Bradley's infamously harsh critique of Shakespeare, for instance).[7] Note also that many works are intended to be appreciated, not by everybody, but only by the initiated few—often those with specialized knowledge (of works alluded to, art history, and so on). Consider the possible scope of the following articulations of the actualist (A) and intentionalist (I) conditions:

(A): x is art $\rightarrow$ x provides for aesthetic experience.

(I): x is art $\rightarrow$ x is intended to provide for aesthetic experience.

Critics of aesthetic theories often seem to believe that if *anyone* fails to find art pleasing, that fact alone falsifies (A), and that if anyone is not included in the class of the intended audience, that falsifies (I). Attributing such implications to aesthetic theories effectively turns them into straw men. We should interpret (A) as requiring only that x provide for *someone's* aesthetic experience, and likewise (I) as requiring only that x be intended to so provide for at least one person.

---

actualist-intentionalist view.

[6] See Stephen Davies, *Definitions of Art* (Ithaca, NY: Cornell University Press, 1991), p. 52; and Robert Stecker, "Definition of Art," in *The Oxford Handbook of Aesthetics*, ed. Jerrold Levinson (Oxford: Oxford University Press, 2003), p. 142. See also Robert Stecker, *Artworks: Definition, Meaning, Value* (University Park, PA: Pennsylvania State University Press, 1997), pp. 35-43.

[7] A.C. Bradley, *Shakespearean Tragedy* (Delhi: Atlantic, 2007), pp. 73 and 75.

I shall defend a form of actualism, as articulated in (A), as a necessary condition for art. (A) seems innocuous on its face; however, critics of the aesthetic approach—and there are many—vehemently reject *any* aesthetic condition, whether (A)-like, (I)-like, or otherwise. Since the objections target (I) as well as (A) brands of aesthetic theory, I will also, in showing the viability of the aesthetic approach generally, discuss plausible ways an intentionalist might respond to these objections.

3. The Proposed Criterion

The main thrust of the objections to most aesthetic theories is that they do not capture a necessary condition for art. But aesthetic theories have been criticized on other grounds as well. There is the concern that no aesthetic condition, even in conjunction with others (such as the artifactuality condition), can prove *sufficient* for art. Suppose we had a drug that produces aesthetic experience—call it *aesthetrix*.[8] One might suppose that the very possibility of such a pharmaceutical must undermine any aesthetic theory of art. As an artifact that produces aesthetic experience and was designed for that purpose, aesthetrix stands as a clear counterexample to both Schlesinger-style (A) accounts and Beardsley-style (I) accounts of art, for the drug is not art, and yet it seems to count as art on either form of aesthetic theory.

A plausible aesthetic criterion must avoid this quandary. Now no one thinks that merely providing for aesthetic experience is sufficient for art. Some non-artworks (such as nautilus shells and sunsets) provide for aesthetic experience, and where intentionalists typically cite the absence of intent so to provide to handle such cases, actualists usually invoke the artifactuality constraint: to count as artwork a thing must be human-made, or better, an artifact, in a suitably broad sense to include both objects and events. We might include such items as driftwood art (and readymades) in the artwork class by identifying the relevant artifact as the *presentation* of the object to the artworld.

---

[8]See, e.g., Stecker, *Artworks*, p. 56. The aesthetrix case is related to, but distinct from, the case of a drug-like work of art, as in Jerrold Levinson, "Defining Art Historically," *British Journal of Aesthetics* 19 (1979), p. 235; and Monroe C. Beardsley, "Redefining Art," in *The Aesthetic Point of View: Selected Essays*, eds. M.J. Wreen and D.M. Callen (Ithaca, NY: Cornell University Press, 1982), pp. 301-2. [Aesthetrix also appears in the novel, Jason Holt, *A Tangent at 3:15* (Dartmouth: H&H Ionic, 2009), pp. 51, 65-71.]

What the aesthetrix case shows is only that the aesthetic criterion needs to be constrained appropriately.

Aesthetrix seems to count against the Schlesinger version of (A) because, in the standard case, the subject of aesthetic experience will also perceive the drug (seeing the pill before swallowing, the liquid before injecting, and so on). Perceiving aesthetrix in this sense obviously has nothing to do with the aesthetically pleasurable effects of the dose. But in art it is precisely perceptual engagement with a work that grounds aesthetic experience of it. To rule out the aesthetrix case, we might add a Dewey-style constraint on how aesthetic experience is provided for: specifically, that it must be provided for by perceptually available properties of the work.[9] "Perceptually available" covers both works (like music) available *in* a sensory modality and works (like literature) available *through* a sensory modality (through vision, say, though the content is not visual). We can avoid the aesthetrix case, then, by specifying the connection between aesthetic experience and the way it is elicited: *An artwork is an artifact that provides for aesthetic experience via perceptually available properties.* This aesthetic criterion, incorporating (A) and similar to Schlesinger's style of actualism, is the one I propose to defend here.

No aesthetic theory would be complete without at least outlining a view of that kind of experience on which it lays so much stress. My account of aesthetic experience stands firmly in a significant tradition in aesthetics, a tradition including—though their views differ widely in crucial respects—the following concepts of aesthetic experience along with their associated proponents: the instructive delight in engaging emotionally cathartic representations (Aristotle); "equipoise" between formal and natural responses (Friedrich Schiller); the "fraternal union" of Apollo and Dionysus (Friedrich Nietzsche); a mingling of the perceptive and sensory pleasures (George Santayana); the special integration of various normal responses into "*an* experience" (John Dewey); the "synaesthesis" of intellectual and emotional responses (I. A. Richards); attentive, unified, and complete pleasurable experience (Beardsley). This tradition may be viewed as arising from Aristotle's rejection of Plato's view of the fundamental, principled, irreconcilable (but superable) antagonism between reason and emotion.

Plato's account strikingly evokes certain work in evolutionary neuropsychology according to which, when the intellect and emotions are engaged—and not severally or jointly quieted—mental life is typified

---

[9] John Dewey, *Art as Experience* (New York: Penguin, 2005), pp. 1-3.

by near constant conflict between the intellectual cortex and the appetitive/emotional diencephalon.[10] Such conflicts include, for example, wanting to do one thing but believing one ought to do something else. Part of what is so phenomenologically special and psychologically valuable about aesthetic experience, in my view, is that it exhibits not only the absence but also the contrary of ordinary mental life so typified: the coherent, mutually reinforcing engagement of both the intellect and the emotions, of both the cortex and the limbic system—*resolutive* experience, I call it.[11] Although Plato does not countenance this type of experience, the tradition in theorizing about aesthetic experience cited above, and extending from Aristotle to the present day, certainly does. For this tradition it is particularly edifying that some recent work in the relatively new field of neuroaesthetics dovetails with it rather remarkably. Of particular interest is the hypothesis that underlying all aesthetic experience is what is known as the peak shift effect, that is, roughly, the tendency to respond more intensely (cortically and subcortically) to "exaggerated" versions of stimuli we normally discriminate.[12]

That said, I should mention some of the assumptions on which I will proceed, as well as certain trends endemic to critics of aesthetic theories. I assume, for instance, that the essentialist program (the attempt to formulate a set of severally necessary and jointly sufficient conditions for art) is a worthwhile project. If not, then at least my efforts will be serviceable, ultimately, as further confirmation of this common-enough suspicion. I also assume that actualism (like intentionalism, for that matter) lays claim to at least a prima facie plausibility, especially in light of the problems besetting its competitors. By and large, critics of actualism tend to be unduly skeptical of the aesthetic in any sense, overly impressed by the avant-garde (or what

---

[10] A.T.W. Simeons, *Man's Presumptuous Brain* (New York: E.P. Dutton, 1961), pp. 40-59.

[11] Jason Holt, "A Comprehensivist Theory of Art," *British Journal of Aesthetics* 36 (1996), p. 427.

[12] V.S. Ramachandran and William Hirstein, "The Science of Art: A Neurological Theory of Aesthetic Experience," *Journal of Consciousness Studies* 6 (1999), p. 18. The notion that all art is caricature seems untenable. How could photorealistic painting count as caricature? The Ramachandran-Hirstein proposal can be interpreted much more charitably, however: A photorealistic painting, by definition, does not caricature the thing depicted, but it does provide what may be called a (fixed) caricature of ordinary (dynamic) experience. In the same way, abstract works that emphasize particular properties—color, texture, shape—caricature ordinary experience in that these properties are not normally emphasized, highlighted, isolated, or framed.

was the avant-garde), and more so by its apparent implications for aesthetic theory.

4. The Anti-Art Objection

The objections to actualism that are my principal focus here purport to show that it is not necessary for art that a work provide for aesthetic experience. Following Stephen Davies, the suspicion underwriting the first objection is that at some stage in the history of art it became possible for art to slough off its original aesthetic function, presuming it had one, and still count as art.[13] In particular, it is alleged that we already have examples of such art among avant-garde, Dadaist work, so-called anti-art, the usual paradigm of which is Marcel Duchamp's readymade *Fountain*, a urinal appropriated for exhibition in a gallery and pseudonymously signed "R. Mutt." Allegedly, the entire point of such anti-art is that it flouts, and was intended to flout, aesthetic expectations and values. Most viewers find such work baffling to say the least, devoid of aesthetic merit, and this is usually taken to mean that the aesthetic condition, ironically for art's sake, has been circumvented.

There are a number of moves the actualist can make in addressing such alleged counterexamples. First, we might simply dismiss the claim that such cases are genuine artworks. While this is a consistent move, the more such cases accrue—and they have accrued significantly—and the more they are so regarded as art by artworld cognoscenti, the less plausible the maneuver seems and the more ad hoc; hence aesthetic theorists, contra Davies, need not deny that such cases are genuine artworks (although a number certainly do deny it). A more contentious line is to say that such cases point at most to minor imperfections in an otherwise useful theory of art, successful in the vast majority of cases.[14]

Admitting such cases as artworks and accepting that they strictly fail to meet the aesthetic condition, the actualist might explain their inclusion in the class of "art" by citing resemblance relations to particular works that meet the condition or kinds of works (i.e., art forms)

---

[13] Davies, *Definitions of Art*, p. 38. Davies refers to the target aesthetic theories as "functionalist."

[14] For further discussion, see Zangwill, "Are There Counterexamples to Aesthetic Theories of Art?"

that usually do. Aside from the general problems associated with resemblance accounts (everything resembles everything else in some respect, and salient resemblances seem to require further explanation that such accounts eschew), the actualist would have to admit that the artwork class is heterogeneous through and through, for whether a work really meets the condition or merely resembles (in the right way) something that does, the piece may count as art. The essentialist project here has defeated itself.

A more plausible tack for the actualist is to accept such cases as artworks and hold that, despite appearances, they meet the actualist condition.[15] Although the urinal used by Duchamp for *Fountain* presumably was not intentionally created to provide for aesthetic experience, and even if Duchamp himself intended, in presenting the urinal to the artworld, to *frustrate* rather than foster aesthetic experience, this does not mean that *Fountain* in fact fails to provide for aesthetic experience. While standard opinion would have it that *Fountain* does not so provide, some people find it to be a delightfully ironic piece, not terribly profound, perhaps, but appreciable nonetheless. It seems that such works *can* indeed provide for aesthetic satisfaction, although admittedly they do so in non-standard ways (whether they ought to is another matter), and that it is in virtue of being ironic in the way it is and commenting on sculpture in the way that it does, that a work like *Fountain* can so provide.[16] Avant-garde and conceptual art can provide for aesthetic experience, even if its way of doing so is less tied to the sensible world than is the case with more traditional artworks. Such properties count as aesthetic in a derivative sense, since they underlie the aesthetic experience that such works provide, and are identified via such provision. If these properties are not aesthetic properties, it is not properties per se but experience alone that puts the *aesthetic* in aesthetic theories of art.

To deny that one could appreciate such works aesthetically in any sense is either psychologically implausible or artistically prejudicial. The untransfigured urinal does not lend itself to such appreciation, and many people simply fail to appreciate *Fountain* post-transfiguration. But this is not terribly significant, as many artworks are not immediately accessible, certainly not to everyone, and this indicates only, as we already knew, that an audience often needs certain degrees and kinds of background knowledge, and perhaps also to be in a certain

---

[15] As is suggested by Stecker, *Artworks*, p. 39.
[16] Ibid., pp. 35 and 62-63.

frame of mind, in order to derive aesthetic experience from seeing some work. What makes a work avant-garde is not that it fails to provide for aesthetic experience at all, but that it provides for aesthetic experience in an unusual way—an unorthodoxy to which many members of an audience will naturally be unaccustomed, and so by default relatively unreceptive.

One concern with this maneuver is that, if such a work as *Fountain* provides for aesthetic experience, it is not clear how anything could then fail to provide for aesthetic experience. Suppose we set aside for the moment the notion of "correct regard," which is particularly difficult to elucidate in any case. Limiting ourselves to perceptible things, it seems that anything could potentially provide for aesthetic experience when viewed in certain conditions, whether standard, somewhat peculiar, or downright bizarre. But while anything *could* provide for aesthetic experience, most things, as a matter of fact, do not. (This is part of the motivation for suggesting that while the aesthetic condition should be retained, it should be retained in a weaker form, disburdened of some of the work to which many would put it.) Bringing back the notion of correct regard, suppose that *Fountain* does, or at least can, provide for aesthetic experience when viewed correctly. (Given variations in human psychology, I take it that regarding a work correctly will be insufficient for having an aesthetic experience of it.) Most things will not provide for aesthetic experience when viewed correctly. Presumably, *Fountain* does, or at least can, provide for aesthetic experience owing in part to the context (being in a gallery) or theoretical background that informs the viewing, differentiating *Fountain* from its indiscernible counterparts. This claim does not imply that it is the institutional or historical context that makes the work a work of art in the first place, although these may be necessary for such works. Either might make a work a salient candidate for aesthetic appreciation without making it art per se. (Usually, by that point the artist has appreciated the work aesthetically already.) If *Fountain* fails so to provide when viewed "correctly," this does not rule out that it so provides *simpliciter*, which is all that the aesthetic view strictly requires. An aesthetic theorist need not be committed to the view that a work of art that provides for aesthetic experience *ought* so to provide. (This matter will be picked up again below.)

It is for the intentionalist that such cases seem particularly difficult, since on the one hand, the urinal Duchamp presented was probably *not* created with the intention to provide for aesthetic experience, and on the other, Duchamp's intentions in presenting it were avowedly, at least to all appearances, anti-aesthetic. It is for exactly this reason that intentionalists such as Beardsley deny that such candidates are genuine artworks, but the intentionalist has some maneuvering room here. For one thing, the urinal itself is not the work, the transfigured urinal is, the urinal-as-transfigured, -as-presented-to-the-artworld. Indeed, *Fountain* is really (arguably) the presentation, by Duchamp, of the urinal to the artworld, in which case the non-aesthetic intentions behind the urinal's manufacture are irrelevant. And what of Duchamp's "anti-aesthetic" intentions? The intentionalist might observe that Duchamp no doubt derived, and intended to derive, an ironic satisfaction from the *succès de scandale* of *Fountain*. It may be argued, then, that Duchamp tried to provide for *his own* aesthetic satisfaction, not only in his choice of materials, but also by using them for shock value, to outrage others by frustrating their hopes to find aesthetic experience in more standard ways.

In order to make this maneuver work, the intentionalist would have to show such ironic satisfaction to constitute, or to be compatible with, genuine aesthetic experience. While Duchamp's satisfaction probably could not count as disinterested, it might nonetheless count, in some sense, as serving his aesthetic interest. Suppose we interpret *Fountain* as the *situation* of Duchamp-presenting-a-urinal-to-the-artworld-as-an-artwork, in which he intended to satisfy his aesthetic interest (perversely, no doubt) *via* the ironic satisfaction of the anti-aesthetic act. On this reading, while the presentation itself was motivated by anti-aesthetic intentions, this is perfectly consistent with Duchamp himself finding the outcome aesthetically piquant (at a meta-level). This is at least somewhat plausible, and although we might never know enough about Duchamp's psychology to confirm such a hypothesis, it does suggest that the infamous readymade may not be the counterexample to intentionalism that it is often taken to be. But even if intentionalism ultimately falls to the anti-art objection (which now seems to require the elusive knowledge that Duchamp did not have such a meta-intention), its actualist cousin remains relatively unscathed.

5. The Circularity Objection

It seems that anti-art can quite plausibly be construed as meeting the actualist condition. The second objection, though, also owing to Stephen Davies, applies even if works like *Fountain* can be so understood. Such works are still important, in Davies's view, since they illustrate how art is conceptually prior to providing for aesthetic experience.[17] If a work like *Fountain* so provides, it does so in part, unlike its untransfigured counterpart, because it has been transfigured. The aesthetic here depends on art, not vice versa, so even if actualism is extensionally adequate (i.e., gets the cases right), it still gets things backwards, and so is ultimately circular.

Here is a reconstruction of Davies's argument:

(1) Actualism implies that something will count as art in part because it provides for aesthetic experience.
(2) Something provides for aesthetic experience in virtue of its aesthetic properties.
(3) A thing's aesthetic properties are those relevant to interpreting it as art.
(4) That a work like *Fountain* is art is relevant to interpreting it, in contrast to its untransfigured counterpart, as art.
(5) Thus, providing for aesthetic experience depends on arthood, not vice versa.
(6) Therefore, aesthetic actualism is circular.[18]

Davies seems to take this objection to apply both to actualism and intentionalism as distinguished here, but it is not particularly problematic for the latter. An intentionalist like Beardsley, whom Davies explicitly targets, could simply say (although this was not Beardsley's actual take on *Fountain*) that one ingredient of the urinal's transfiguration is the intention that it provide, in some sense, for aesthetic experience, and this intention is necessary for art even if being art in the first place is necessary for a work like *Fountain actually* to provide for aesthetic experience.

The standard actualist reply is to deny (2), at least as Davies construes it.[19] On such a reading, Davies thinks the actualist is committed to the view that *all* of a thing's aesthetic properties figure into

---

[17]Davies, *Definitions of Art*, pp. 66-67.

[18]This is adapted from Anderson, "Aesthetic Concepts of Art," p. 75.

[19]Such a reply is suggested in Stecker, *Artworks*, pp. 62-63; and Anderson, "Aesthetic Concepts of Art," pp. 76-77.

its providing for aesthetic experience, and by extension its arthood. If we are forced to accept that being art at all is an aesthetic property, then the actualist can simply deny that all of a work's aesthetic properties figure into its arthood. That *Fountain* is about the artworld, is seemingly ironic, and provokes questions, say, about the history of sculpture—these are the properties that help *Fountain* provide for aesthetic experience and elevate the urinal to arthood. Being art is not. In fact, we may well doubt whether being art is an aesthetic property at all, except perhaps in the trivial way that knowing that something is art relieves one of the possible burden of having to determine as much.

Thus, while the standard rejection of (2) is presumably sufficient, we might also plausibly object to (3) and (4), which seem to presuppose (and thus commit the actualist, if not Davies himself, to) the controversial view that aesthetic properties, those relevant to interpreting something as art, attach strictly to artifacts (more strictly still, to art) and not, for instance, to beautiful things in nature: sunsets, nautilus shells, erosion patterns, and so on, except perhaps in a derivative sense. A more plausible view would be that aesthetic properties are those relevant to providing for aesthetic experience, or perhaps those that are relevant to interpreting something as if it *were* art. Naturally, we need not deny sunsets and nautilus shells original (i.e., non-derivative) aesthetic properties to exclude them from the class of artworks.

6. The Bad-Art Objection

A longstanding objection to actualism concerns its apparent collapse of the fact/value distinction. If part of what it takes to be art at all is that a work manages to provide for aesthetic experience, then in virtue of such success, any bona fide artwork will have at least some aesthetic value, however minimal. While this maps well onto the evaluative sense of art in certain approbative predications (as in "*That's a work of art!*"), it appears to leave anything like a purely classificatory, descriptive sense of "art" nowhere. For this reason, actualism may seem to fail to provide the foundational sort of theory that we are really after—a theory of *art*. In its more recent guises, the objection runs something like this: Intuitively, there are some artworks devoid of aesthetic merit, which do not satisfy aesthetic interest. They are thoroughly bad pieces. On the actualist view, though, any work that counts as art is *not* devoid of aesthetic merit. Thus, actualism is false.[20]

It should be noted that despite certain allegations to the contrary (e.g., Davies's critique of Beardsley),[21] intentionalist theories of art are immune to this objection. A work may have been created with the intention that it provide for aesthetic experience without that intention in any way being fulfilled. (Beardsley was quite explicit about this commitment, and it is a mystery why Davies criticizes him on this basis.) In such a case, the intention to produce the work is fulfilled but the intention to have it produce aesthetic experience is not. Bad art poses no problem here.

The actualist can adopt several different strategies in responding to the bad-art objection. One is simply to bite the bullet and insist that "art" properly has only a value-laden sense. The motivation for such a move might be to preserve the straightforward account of aesthetic value so often prized by actualists. To account for the intuition that there are thoroughly bad works, the actualist might say a number of things, for instance, that such works count as art by dint of resemblance-relations borne by effective works, although here again we abandon essentialism. Alternatively, it might be urged that the merit of bad works, while real, is negligible, and so for practical purposes only, if not in truth, nil. Discounting the statistically negligible in this sense is not an arbitrary matter but, in fact, a principled one. Another point is that bad works—really, really *bad* works (the poetry of William McGonagall comes to mind)—might be seen as succeeding, on some level, in spite of themselves, because of their very badness, almost as if they're so bad, they're good—that is, aesthetically appreciable at a meta-level for their thoroughgoing first-order badness. Especially in such cases as McGonagall's, it is somewhat intuitive that perfectly awful works satisfy the aesthetic interest in some sense, often in stark contrast with the artist's intentions. McGonagall's verse is very amusing, albeit unintentionally, and it certainly sells well. Still, it would be difficult to justify this view. Since I am not claiming that it is true, much less staking much on the claim, perhaps it is best left alone. We might observe, even so, that thoroughly bad works also serve to contrast with, and thus heighten our appreciation of, good art, and so do provide for a kind of appreciation, not only in themselves but also,

---

[20] Davies, *Definitions of Art*, p. 76; and Stecker, *Artworks*, p. 39.

[21] Davies, *Definitions of Art*, pp. 62-77.

indirectly, of other work.

One may doubt whether such lines of reply will succeed, although they might nonetheless merit further inquiry. Some artworks, it would seem, merely leave us cold, are not ironically appreciable, and need not necessarily figure into our appreciation of quality work. Even if they did, this is at best a Procrustean form of what most actualists intend. Still, the notion of being practically devoid of aesthetic merit if not in truth has a certain degree of plausibility, echoing to a certain extent the idea that bad works *merely* serve a function while good works serve it *well*. It seems that thoroughly bad works are akin to, say, thoroughly bad can openers, the successful use of which causes too much strain and bother, or the doorstop that must precariously be balanced to do its job and is easy to dislodge. While such things work, they do not work well. The sensible thing may be to revise one's preferences (not bothering with the art, going without tuna, letting the door close) or procure items that work well to use instead (better art, a better can opener, a better doorstop). A threshold problem may be looming here, but this may indicate little more than that the working/working well distinction is a somewhat vague one, as is the bald/hirsute distinction or the red/orange distinction.

Another, perhaps more radical move is to abandon the unnecessary link between something's providing for aesthetic experience and its being of aesthetic value. No doubt aesthetic experience is of psychological value, and can be had in the absence of anything that merits such response. Consider, then, different positions on the metaphysical status of aesthetic value. If we are realists, and suppose such values to be mind-independent, a work may provide for aesthetic experience even if it ought not to as a matter of fact. If instead we suppose aesthetic norms to be embodied by something like David Hume's standard of taste,[22] in this case too a work may so provide in ways not sanctioned by the standard. From a relativist perspective, a bad work is one that, say, leaves *me* cold, though it may still count as art (objectively) because, as matter of fact, it works for someone else. The only real problem here would be if we had a democratic "standard" of value somewhere in between Hume's and the relativist's, in which case a work's effectiveness for anyone at any time would count as some measure of aesthetic value. But not only is such a view implausible

---

[22]David Hume, "Of the Standard of Taste," in *Aesthetics: A Critical Anthology*, eds. George Dickie, Richard Sclafani, and Ronald Roblin (New York: St. Martin's Press, 1989), pp. 242-53.

on its face, it would seem readily handled by one of the responses suggested above (biting the bullet, the working/working well distinction, discounting the negligible, or some combination of these).

The intentionalist is still immune to the bad-art objection, and anyone inclined to press for a truly democratic standard of aesthetic value has to overcome a rather heavy burden of proof.

7. The Many-Roles Objection

The next objection turns on the idea that art has a great variety of functions and these functions evolve over time. We might cite the fact that art had a much more religious function in the Middle Ages than it does in the more secularized artworld of today, that art tends to be more politically and socially conscious than it used to be, that certain art forms, like painting, which once had the function of representing the world, have come, in more or less recent times, to admit of other purposes, as is seen in such traditions as abstract expressionism. If art has such ever-evolving functions, it would seem that no single function, such as providing for aesthetic experience, is essential.[23] Any function one might point to as plausibly essential in point of fact or principle might come off as exceptionable. Indeed, if providing for aesthetic experience seems essential to art, this is because other comparably plausible functions, such as expressing emotion or presenting formally interesting stimuli, are being ignored.

It should be obvious that this objection targets both actualist and intentionalist species of aesthetic theory. In terms of the dynamic pluralist picture offered here, artists' intentions and purposes would seem no less varying, no less evolving, than the panoply of psychological and cultural roles played by artwork post-production. It should also be clear that this view is substantially correct in character if not in implication. It cannot be denied that artists' creative intentions and the further purposes for which they create, the techniques they employ and the styles they exhibit, the media they use and the manners of use, the character of their work and its repercussions, both psychological and cultural, are all subject to great variation and change over time.

The burden on the actualist is to account for these seemingly obvious facts in a way that staves off the apparent implication that art has no essential function. As it turns out, this is not a particularly

---

[23]Stecker, *Artworks*, p. 50.

onerous task. Providing for aesthetic experience is multiply realizable if anything is. In implementing the aesthetic, there are obviously going to be various ways of getting the job done, different inputs (conditions of creation) yielding different outputs (consequences of creation), even if at some abstract level the conditions and consequences are uniform. This is so even if we limit ourselves to a single aesthetic property (one purely formal property, say). While artworks may function in many ways which have nothing to do with their being art (e.g., being used as doorstops), the variety of functions they have *qua* art will be variations in the *proaesthetic* means to providing for aesthetic experience, or the *peraesthetic* effects of such provision, if there is indeed such variety. Suppose a poet expresses emotion in writing a poem that garners critical praise, while a painter exhibits a formally interesting canvas that fetches a staggering price from an appreciative collector. Variation in these scenarios is a matter not of not providing for aesthetic experience, but rather in the proaesthetic means (expressivist or formalist) and in the peraesthetic effects (cachet versus wealth) of such provision.

Of course, I am giving the objection the benefit of the doubt here. The point is not that there *is* such variety in, say, what I am calling the proaesthetic means, but rather that if there were such variety, as the objection suggests there is, this would not entail that the aesthetic condition fails. The only implication would be that there are various ways to get done the same basic job of providing for aesthetic experience.

8. The Denied-Aesthetic Objection

The last objection I will deal with in any detail is that while actualism posits aesthetic experience as what is provided for by art, there is no such thing as aesthetic experience, nothing distinctively aesthetic about experiences so labeled. At the core of the objection is the notion that aesthetic experience is at best a heterogeneous kind, ultimately unreal.

There are two prongs to this objection. First, it has been claimed that while a lot of art provides audiences with some experiences that involve some measure of emotional and cognitive—one might say intellectual—response, some nominally aesthetic experiences appear to be of a purely sensuous nature (as when one appreciates the mere texture of a sculpture, say).[24] Similarly, it has been claimed that alongside genuinely appreciative experiences, aesthetic experience may include mere detection of or attention to certain properties of a work (formal, expressive, aesthetic) without concomitant appreciation.[25] Second, it has been claimed that with most aesthetic experiences, the intellectual and emotional responses involved vary too widely for there to be anything common and peculiar to the class.[26] I will defend the concept of aesthetic experience as a uniform, genuine kind from the somewhat plausible, but ultimately answerable, suggestion that aesthetic experience is too varied for this to be the case.

Skepticism about the aesthetic generally is elaborated, it seems, from persuasive critiques of such posits as an aesthetic mode of perception, the aesthetic attitude, and a distinct aesthetic faculty. Aesthetic experience need not, however, be cashed out in such tendentious ways. The irony here is that many of those who object to the aesthetic in any sense, on the grounds that it is a disjunctive kind (and so arguably, in a sense, not a *real* kind), are happy to give disjunctive but avowedly realist theories of art (where a kind—*artwork* in this case—is held to be real even though there are alleged to be no necessary and sufficient conditions for it). The problem, if it is a problem, applies equally to both or to neither.

It should be clear that this objection poses less of an immediate problem for intentionalism. After all, one can intend to create a work that provides for aesthetic experience even if, as a matter of fact, there is no such thing, just as one can intend to hunt unicorns, worship Odin, or discover the last digit in *pi*. But there is a difficulty lurking in the wings. As intentionalism is consistent with anti-realism about aesthetic experience, it might turn out that in order to make art, or in order to do so rationally, artists must never be disabused of the "beautiful lie" (rather than noble lie) that such experiences exist.

Turning to actualism, in responding to the claim that some aesthetic experiences are purely sensuous, we might maintain either that such experiences are not in any strict sense aesthetic, or that they are not purely sensuous. We might echo Immanuel Kant and insist that these pleasures are too base to take the stamp of genuine aesthetic experience.[27] Aesthetic experience is something we often value over

[24]Davies, *Definitions of Art*, p. 59; and Stecker, *Artworks*, p. 37.

[25]Noël Carroll, "Art and the Domain of the Aesthetic," *British Journal of Aesthetics* 40 (2000), p. 207.

[26]Davies, *Definitions of Art*, pp. 59-60; and Stecker, *Artworks*, p. 36.

[27]Immanuel Kant, *Critique of Judgment*, trans. Werner S. Pluhar (Indianapolis,

and above the purely sensuous. For the sake of the aesthetic we often forgo the instant gratification of the sensuous. Another tack is to claim that it is not aesthetic but purely sensuous experience that is the fiction. As pleasurable, sensuous experience involves the emotions, and so seemingly must also involve subconscious cognition, as when figures and faces and shapes generally exhibit the golden ratio, which we are more or less hardwired to find attractive, irrespective of whether such knowledge is ever made explicit.

Even so, the term "aesthetic" is sometimes used—elastically—to underscore the delight we sometimes take in certain sensations for their own sake. Misuse of the term sometimes involves confusing the character of the object of experience with that of the experience itself. One can experience artwork, even pleasurably, without the experience having to have an aesthetic character at all (think of nude studies). An experience *of* an aesthetic object, or even of its aesthetically relevant properties, need not be an aesthetic experience. Sensuous experience of artwork, or detecting and attending to features that would be relevant to its active appreciation, might in fact lead to, accompany, or be part of aesthetic experience, but it might just as well not, and so its potential involvement in aesthetic experience does not imply that there is anything aesthetic about such sensuous, attentive, or detective experience on its own.

As for the problem of variety, I will take an example that is oversimplified but nonetheless illustrative. Suppose a tragedy makes me sad and makes me think seriously about dire fate, while a comedy makes me happy and makes me think lightheartedly about lucky coincidence. What could these experiences possibly have in common? Again, we might follow Kant, according to whom, very roughly, aesthetic experience consists in free play between the faculties of the imagination and the understanding, regardless of the *content* of either of these faculties.[28] In terms of this discussion, while my tragedy-response and my comedy-response may have nothing in common intellectually or emotionally, this does not mean that the two have nothing peculiarly aesthetic in common. Not only do they both involve the intellect and the emotions but, more strikingly, their variety in content does not rule out the possibility that in both cases there is the same type of *relation* between intellect and emotion, one that overarches admittedly variable content. Above I characterized the relation, and the experience,

IN: Hackett, 1987), sec. 7, pp. 31-32.
    [28]Ibid., sec. 9, p. 62.

in terms of the *resolution* of conflict between intellect and emotion, not the quelling of either, but the coherent engagement of both. If mental life is characterized by such conflict typically, this would help explain the psychological value of art.[29]

What I am suggesting here is that at the appropriate level of abstraction, there is something common and peculiar to the class of aesthetic experiences. At the very least I have shown that this particular objection does not suffice to show that such a theory of aesthetic experience cannot be defended. Sensuous experience can be dismissed as non-aesthetic or as implicitly impure, whereas detecting or attending to aesthetic properties, though clearly *of* the aesthetic, are insufficient for aesthetic experience. Plus, judicious abstraction to common and peculiar relations between mental faculties takes care of the problem of variable content. Thus a univocal, robust notion of aesthetic experience can be preserved.

9. Conclusion

Critics and advocates alike might see what I have attempted here as taking the teeth out of aesthetic theories by delegating less work to the aesthetic condition than is standard, suggesting that we might have to abandon the erstwhile strong link between actualism and aesthetic (though not psychological) value. But abandoning this link would only be anathema to the aesthetic approach in general if the value of aesthetic experience were not significantly bound up with human psychology, and if human psychology were not sufficiently varied to allow for different permissible (if not all strictly correct) responses to art, or relatedly if one could infer something about the objective value of art from the simple fact that someone finds it valuable in a certain way (this simple fact nonetheless being necessary, according to the actualist, for art). Such a condition is in concert with the aesthetic approach in general, not only for preserving the link between art and the aesthetic, but also for suggesting (if not implying) the form a reasonable (if reductive) account of aesthetic value might take. In its most defensible form, actualism does less work than otherwise, but in avoiding the most virulent attacks on aesthetic theories, it does enough.

I have proposed an aesthetic criterion for art motivated by a de-

---

[29] Holt, "A Comprehensivist Theory of Art," p. 427.

fense of the (A) condition (actualism) from the key—and often thought devastating—objections levied against aesthetic theories. These objections, I argue, can successfully be parried without compromising the objectives of the aesthetic approach to defining art. At least none of the objections seems now to have scored a very palpable hit.

6 NEUROAESTHETICS AND PHILOSOPHY

Introduction

Neuroaesthetics studies and provides frameworks for interpreting brain structures and functions of creative artists and receptive audiences. As characteristically part of or accompanying the production and enjoyment of artworks, aesthetic experience is one particularly rewarding type of experience in which personal and theoretical interest are understandable. This paper aims to identify the potential of neuroaesthetics to contribute to philosophically motivated investigations of art and to critically evaluate and undermine skepticism about such contributions. In particular, it is proposed that aesthetic experience involves a distinctive corticolimbic response, that such experience is therefore testable and may be found even with so-called anti-art, and that its value consists in resolution of conflict between the higher cortex and limbic system generated by the evolution of the former.

The term "neuroaesthetics" (minus the "a" and hyphenated) appears to have been coined by the neuroscientist Semir Zeki (1999). Published the very same year as Zeki's *Inner Vision* was a special issue of the *Journal of Consciousness Studies* whose target article, by the neuroscientist V.S. Ramachandran and philosopher William Hirstein (1999), fomented enough controversy to spawn two special issue sequels. Although the field has grown and developed significantly since then (e.g., see Skov & Vartanian, 2009), the focus here will be on these earlier attempts because of their comparatively broad scope and clearer relevance to the skepticism addressed. Still, it is neuroaesthetics generally that is central here, as both these illustrative cases appear to justify philosophical skepticism about neuroaesthetics yet reveal the potential contribution of neuroaesthetics, in some form or the other, to the philosophy of art. Such use seems consistent with Ramachandran's (2001) own assessment (p. 28) of "The Science of Art" as suggesting the form a final theory might take. The argument is that not only does skepticism about neuroaesthetics prove false, its target might yield the necessary bridge between traditional philosophy of art and a robust, insightful, truly interdisciplinary aesthetics. Art history is tangential to this direction of argument, but the history of philosophical aesthetics, of art theory in this sense, is not. This is not to say that anthropology and art history, among other areas, will not contribute to a complete theoretical picture of art (see, for example, respectively, Dissanayake, 1995; Onians, 2007). However, the focus in this article is on the particular, often divisive tension between philosophy and neuroscience in theorizing about art.

The controversy spurred by Ramachandran and Hirstein (1999) among some philosophers had a threefold cause: the authors' temerity in suggesting that theory of art might benefit from neuroscience (and might be stymied by neglecting it), comfort in making sweeping claims of perhaps uncertain scope under the heading "8 laws of aesthetic experience" (which became 10 laws in Ramachandran, 2003), and apparent naïveté in attempting the task without perhaps knowing enough about art. E.H. Gombrich's (2000) commentary is a single 12-line paragraph, cuttingly dismissive: "Even a fleeting visit to one of the great museums might serve to convince the authors that few of the exhibits conform to the laws of art they postulate" (p. 17). The first special issue contained understandably eager and wide-ranging objections (Baars, 1999; Gregory, 1999; Kindy, 1999; Lanier, 1999; Mangan, 1999; Martindale, 1999; Mitter, 1999; Wallen, 1999), which prompted clarifications and refinements (e.g., Ramachandran, 2001; 2003). Yet others have suggested that there remain untapped riches in the original paper. For instance, Tyler (1999) rightly observes that the principle of perceptual problem-solving (one of the 8 laws), though glossed over to the point of neglect in "The Science of Art," is perhaps the principle that might be of most interest to artists themselves; in perceptual problem-solving there is an isomorphism between the artist's process of creating the visual "puzzle" of the work and the viewer's experience of "solving" it. It is in such a spirit that this article is written.

The importance of exploring the potential of neuroaesthetics for aiding understanding of not only aesthetic experience, which is plausible enough on its face, but the nature of art, which might not be as plausible a connection, is reflected in the present state of the art of philosophical aesthetics. After Danto's (1964; 1981) landmark work on indiscernibles, which focused on what distinguishes art (e.g., Andy Warhol's *Brillo Boxes*) from perceptually indistinguishable non-art (e.g., ordinary Brillo boxes), attention shifted away from the earlier view that art is indefinable to theories purporting to give necessary and sufficient conditions for art by focusing on the *relations* between artist and artwork in the first instance and artwork and audience in the second.

Although objections have since resurfaced (e.g., Gaut, 2000) to the view that it is these relations, in some form or the other, in which the essence of art is located, present theories of art proceed for the most part on this assumption. Disputes in art theory center instead on the *kinds* of relation on which art status depends: whether (a) historical, (b) institutional, or (c) functional (for "functional" read "psycholog-ical," and for "psychological" read "aesthetic"). Historical and insti-tutional views—which define art in terms of earlier artworks and the institution of the artworld, respectively—are apparently inadequate not only for standard reasons (circularity, nominalism, etc.), but also because proponents of such views (e.g., Davies, 1991; Stecker, 1997), to handle these objections, have had to effectively abandon necessary and sufficient conditions for art by giving alternative, ad hoc accounts in problematic cases (specifically the case of first art, which lacks his-torical precedent and precedes the artworld itself). As importantly, appealing to art's psychological/aesthetic properties opens the door to explanations of *how* historical precedence and artworld agency oc-cur (see Iseminger, 2004). The stakes, then, are far greater than what natural curiosity there might be, and should be, in the "mere" neuro-logical profile of art. If psychological/aesthetic accounts are the most promising among competing theories of art, then the contribution of neuroaesthetics will be absolutely crucial in discovering the underlying nature of aesthetic experience and in finally uncovering the nature of art itself.

The next section will outline different sources of skepticism about the potential role of neuroaesthetics in contributing significantly to the philosophy of art, showing how scientists' ventures into art theory seem to confirm these suspicions, and how philosophers themselves likewise have fallen short (shared narrowness of vision being to blame). There will follow an account of how Ramachandran and Hirstein's proposal, despite its apparent problems, dovetails elegantly, and to mutual benefit, with a certain long-standing tradition in philosophical aesthetics. It will also be argued that this blend of neuroscience and traditional aesthetics has the potential to defeat the skeptic on all three fronts (the relevance of neuroscience to art theory, the existence of aesthetic experience as such, the central importance of aesthetic experience to the philosophy of art), thus tackling the nature of art from a wide interdisciplinary stance.

Narrow Vision?

Whether expressly so or merely by implication, many philosophers are skeptical about whether neuroaesthetics has anything significant to offer theories of art or aesthetic experience (such as Carroll, 2003; Currie, 2003; Davies, 1991; Dickie, 2000; Seeley, 2006). There are three types of skepticism about the role neuroaesthetics might play in contributing anything to the philosophy of art. This section will distinguish these three forms of skepticism and show how scientists' ventures into art theory, and philosophers' ventures into science for art theory's sake, in some cases seem to confirm such skepticism. It will also argue that this perspective is rather short-sighted.

The most obvious type of skepticism relevant here stems from broad misgivings many philosophers have had about whether empirical questions or findings can have any bearing on philosophical theory: the view that philosophy is strictly an armchair discipline. Although this "resistance to facts" seems to have been overcome in the philosophy of the natural and social sciences, traditional domains in the arts and humanities—philosophy of art, saliently—have proved more resistant, probably because—the "social" in "social sciences" aside—of the suspicion that truly and distinctively cultural phenomena lie beyond the long arm of scientific reach, that scientific approaches are too low-level to reveal what is desirable to know about art and aesthetic response (Currie, 2003; Dickie, 2000; Mitter, 1999; Wallen, 1999). This seems a mild version of the unfortunate trend now popular in the humanities to consider *everything*, and not just everything social, "social." The trend is evident even when it comes to pure descriptive questions such as "What is art?" because such questions in particular often seem tightly if not inextricably tied up with questions of value, not just psychological value but cultural meaning. Whether or not "art" has a pure descriptive sense, the banishment of science from this domain is held to be a principled one, Zeki's neologism "neuroaesthetics" an affront, on this view, to good sense and good taste.

A second type of skepticism derives, not from the belief that science is ill-equipped or intrusive, but rather from antirealism about aesthetic experience. Perhaps science can reveal a lot about art, perhaps not, but allowing that one should quantify over experiences (after all, one might deny that consciousness exists), aspersions have been cast on the very term "aesthetic," because, it is argued, it fails to designate a legitimate experiential kind, as there seems to be nothing common and peculiar to aesthetic experiences (Davies, 1991; Dickie, 1964). Often marshaled against the aesthetic are various arguments to the effect that the notion of a disinterested aesthetic attitude, a peculiar aesthetic faculty, or a distinctive aesthetic kind of perception, are at best irremediably vague, at middling susceptible to standard sorts of argument-from-oddness objections, and at worst, most simply, incoherent. The usual diagnosis (though note Shusterman's, 1997, cogent reply to such concerns) is that the very concept of the aesthetic is the culprit, the prescription to eliminate it from strict discourse about art, and the implication a fortiori that neuroaesthetics on pain of recasting is a nonstarter.

A third type of skepticism might allow scientific input into the realm of art theory, and might even include the aesthetic as a legitimate type of experience, but nonetheless takes its cue from rival perspectives on art: historicism, institutionalism, as well as antiessentialism (the view that art cannot be defined). If any of these is correct, and the first two can withstand the objections mentioned earlier, including obviation of the "explanatory reduction" briefly sketched, then neuroaesthetics will have little to say about the nature of art. Note that it could still contribute much, more narrowly, to theories of the aesthetic, in which case it would still be a worthy, if more modest, endeavor. It would be appropriate to note that historicist and institutional views of art are often motivated by a rejection of the aesthetic as a unifying, universal concept for art (see Davies, 1991, for the general concern, Brown & Dissanayake, 2009, for the neuroaesthetics-specific concern). Cases of the so-called anti-art, or antiaesthetic art, the paradigm case of which is Duchamp's *Fountain* (a urinal pseudonymously signed and presented in an art gallery), which allegedly counts as art and flouts the aesthetic, are usually adduced to show how art and the aesthetic pull apart.

Such skepticism about the potential contribution of neuroaesthetics to the philosophy of art finds some support in certain work by scientists treading in such unfamiliar territory. Take Zeki's (1999) *Inner Vision*, which was mentioned at the outset and in which such claims are made (the first figuratively apt, perhaps, but quite literally put) that artists *are* neuroscientists (pp. 2, 10) and that *all* art aims at providing knowledge (pp. 9-10). Zeki also goes to great lengths in establishing, for instance, that without the brain area responsible for color vision (V4), one cannot appreciate the color of a painting, that without the brain area responsible for perceiving motion (MT or V5), one cannot fully appreciate kinetic artworks like mobiles. To a philosopher of art, no doubt, such elaborations come off as misguided in the first case and rather trivial (not neuroscientifically trivial but, given the neuroscience, aesthetically trivial) in the second. As will be seen, similar concerns are raised likewise by some of the assertions made by Ramachandran and Hirstein.

To forestall needless proliferation of instances, let these suffice for now, save to observe that in most cases, and this applies no less to philosophers who draw on, or simply give lip service to, scientific research, here lies an unfortunate narrowness of vision. Even where more interesting and useful work is done (in linking visual ambiguity with interpretive openness, for instance), not only is there an excess of bottom-up material, it comes off as omitting the "up." Some top-down work, or at least top-with-an-eye-to-down work, seems necessary, as most interdisciplinary inquiry in this area, whether by scientists or philosophers, concerns chiefly visual art and the visual system, with scarcely a mention or other (nonvisual) art forms, other sense modalities, or the possibility of commonalities in aesthetic response *across* various art forms. Of course, music will excite the auditory cortex rather than the visual, but what might responses to music and responses to painting have in common, perhaps in different cortices, perhaps in common structures further down the line? Whither breadth of vision?—or breadth beyond vision? Perhaps surprisingly, in the answer to this question one begins to glimpse the greatest contribution to the philosophy of art that neuroaesthetics might make.

A Tradition's Cutting Edge

This section will directly engage Ramachandran and Hirstein's "The Science of Art" (1999) as an illustrative case to argue that, its apparent shortcomings aside, neuroaesthetics meshes well at an abstract level with aesthetics of a more traditional philosophical style, and so might just provide insight into not only the underlying nature of aesthetic experience but also the ultimate nature of art itself. Discussion will continue to be confined to chiefly philosophical concerns.

On the surface, despite one of the authors being a philosopher, "The Science of Art" reads like many other attempts by scientists to engage in art theory. There are the expected problematic pronouncements, such as, without qualification, that all art is beautiful (without disambiguating the beauty of the depiction from the beauty of the thing depicted)—which is suggested (Ramachandran & Hirstein, 1999) if not explicitly made—and stranger, that all art is caricature, without addressing such obvious counterexamples as, say, photorealistic painting. The puzzling caricature principle derives from emphasis placed throughout the article on what is called the "peak shift" effect, a tendency to respond more intensely to exaggerated versions of stimuli that humans are geared, through habit or reward, to discriminate typically. If a person is discriminating rectangles from squares, say, they will tend to respond much more intensely to an elongated (thus exaggerated) rectangle. The fact that stimulus novelty generates such response stresses the importance of the internal mechanisms involved.

The peak shift effect is labeled one of the "laws of aesthetic experience," along with perceptual grouping and binding, attention allocation, contrast extraction, perceptual problem-solving, the generic viewpoint principle, and—odd as these may seem in rounding out the list—metaphor, and symmetry (repetition/rhythm and balance are added to the slightly altered list of Ramachandran, 2003). The diversity of this list, the non-lawlike formulations of its "laws," and their ambiguous scope, have been cause for concern, although appreciated in some cases, among philosophers of a certain mindset.

Although these more philosophical misgivings do not scratch the surface of criticisms made from other disciplines (as one may reasonably expect), the focus here will be on the more philosophically central issues. Many of the claims about which philosophers would rightly be prima facie skeptical can actually be given more deservedly defensible interpretations. First, the claim that all art is beautiful will strike many philosophers of art as absurd—when "beautiful" is interpreted naturalistically—because where much art depicts the beautiful, much of it also depicts the ugly, and so forth: Botticelli's *Venus* is one thing, Goya's *Saturn* another. Add to this that much postmodern art deliberately flouts any traditional notion of beauty (Western or Eastern), and it is clear why many philosophers will too quickly dismiss the claim that all art is beautiful. However, if art is deemed beautiful in the sense that it provokes pleasurable aesthetic response, then the claim seems much more plausible, and is not so easy to dismiss. Still, Ramachandran and Hirstein seem to prefer the more standard interpretation of "beautiful," which remains open to this criticism except insofar as, despite their claims to universality, their proposals are meant to apply only to beautiful art in the narrower sense.

Second, the caricature principle (that all art is caricature) could be given a similarly charitable reading. Abstract art is a caricature insofar as, by definition, it is abstracted from, hence serves in that sense as a caricature of, ordinary experience and representations of it. Not so with realistic representations, however, as a photorealistic painting is certainly no caricature in the way that most political cartoons are. In fact, Ramachandran (2003) is quite explicit about realistic representation, in a snapshot, say, ruling the representation out of the artwork class. The implications for a host of realistic artworks—much artistic photography, photorealistic painting, and so on—is distressing. It seems Ramachandran here sells his theory short, in that realistic depictions can be interpreted, and quite straightforwardly, as caricatures in some relevant sense. Take photorealistic painting. Though not a typical caricature, to be sure, a photorealistic painting is importantly different, "abstracted," from ordinary experience in one very important way: by freezing time. In presenting a frozen timeslice of a limited perspective, the visual display in a photorealistic painting has, in a sense, made a caricature of the depicted scene, which does not really stand still (and is not really flat, either). Realism should apply as much in four dimensions as in three.

Although such an interpretation is possible, it is perhaps implausible to attribute it to the authors who, after all, sought to provoke further discussion more than settle theoretical matters outright. Even so, it is instructive to realize that "The Science of Art" might have better mileage than Ramachandran and Hirstein had hoped. Clearly, some of its provocative claims have yet to be fully appreciated (even by Ramachandran himself) for their defensibility, as has been shown, or their potential philosophical significance, as will be shown.

Two important themes emerge from the provocative discussion in "The Science of Art." The first theme is well expressed in the article's guiding question: "Might there be some sort of universal rule or 'deep structure' underlying all [aesthetic] experience? . . . What is the brain circuitry involved?" (p. 16). Not only does this question give the right breadth of perspective so desperately lacking in much work of this ilk, it indicates that certain crucial questions about the aesthetic (whether there *is* such a thing, for one) might just admit of answers that can be sought empirically, getting beyond what often appears as intuition-haggling or question-begging in the philosophy of art. (Ramachandran, 2003, seems to think that philosophy is inherently this way, and so cannot discover universal laws, much less testable ones—otherwise philosophers would simply be scientists, as though the philosophy of art were only good science or bad art history.)

The second theme, an implicit one, is an apparent commonality lurking beneath the "8 laws" that begins, when abstractly formulated, to resemble far more familiar aesthetic theory than may at first appear: in aesthetic experience (as in peak shift) there is a special, more intense response than in ordinary experience, a relationship of special reinforcement between distinct parts of the brain: the limbic system (spatially lower, evolutionarily older, more emotional) and the cortex (spatially higher, evolutionarily newer, more intellectual: Holt, 1996; 2010). This perspective helps explain the value of aesthetic experience, especially against a background commitment to the hypothesis that the explosive evolution of the neocortex resulted in the human psyche being typified by deep conflict between reason and emotion (Koestler, 1967; Simeons, 1961).

The notion of aesthetic experience as consisting in a distinctive corticolimbic relation, though suggested in "The Science of Art," is not given much notice there, even though the idea suggests much greater universality—which the authors prize above all—than the 8 (and later 10) principles themselves. Nor is mention made that this unified view, rather than competing, in fact complements more traditional art theory, particularly a certain tradition in theorizing about aesthetic experience, a tradition that can be seen in Beardsley (1981, p. 552) acknowledging the debt of his account to that of, among others, Richards, Ogden, and Wood (1925, pp. 75-77), where aesthetic experience is viewed as a harmonious "synaesthesis" between the intellect and the emotions. These 20th-century analytic philosophers' views find precedence in 19th-century Continental philosophy: Schiller's (2004) notion of aesthetic experience as "equipoise" between rational and natural impulses (pp. 74-75, 90), and even Nietzsche's

(1967) idea of the "fraternal union" of Apollo and Dionysus (p. 132) can be seen as a similar view in more symbolic garb. The corticolimbic relationship suggested by "The Science of Art," then, appears to account, even if not intended to, for how aesthetic experience, as given by such philosophical descriptions, is implemented in the brain—again, a complementary, not a competing, approach.

This complementarity with philosophy is encouraging, revealing neuroaesthetics to be far broader, and far more powerful, than it often appears and its critics suppose. Not only is there the potential for a unified theory of aesthetic experience across sense modalities here, the hypothesis of aesthetic experience having a corticolimbic signature implies the possibility of testing for such experience, even in the case of so-called anti-art, which might be found to elicit such a response *despite* the artist's intentions. The corticolimbic signature of aesthetic experience might turn out to be some unique kind of self-reinforcing thalamocortical feedback loop. Although at this point the discussion is admittedly speculative, it should be noted that this is where new neuroaesthetic lab work should take up the slack. It should also be noted, however, that this proposal already has some intuitive plausibility, coheres with an established philosophical tradition in aesthetics, gives a direction for further empirical research (including suggestive hypotheses), and helps arm the philosopher and neuroaesthetician alike against the skeptic.

Consider how this perspective on complementarity suggests replies to the various forms of skepticism outlined earlier. To the resistance to scientific intrusion in this domain, it might be observed that the scientific branch of neuroaesthetics represents, not a threat to aesthetics, but a potentially fruitful and, in a certain sense, badly needed partnership. The low-level neuroscience will provide the means to flesh out, refine, challenge, and vindicate certain accounts of aesthetic experience, introspectively plausible and art-theoretically sensitive. Without neuroaesthetics, the philosophy of art is fleshless; without philosophy, the science of art is blind.

Skepticism about aesthetic experience as such, which is usually grounded in the intuition that responses to art vary far too widely for there to be anything distinctively "aesthetic" about them, can be parried by noting three things: first, that the postulated "deep structure" of aesthetic experience would, if vindicated, unify aesthetic experience without need of surface transparency; second, that the relational/multiple faculties model already allows for intellectual and emotional content in aesthetic experience to vary as widely as possible without sacrificing a commitment to unity in the relation *between* the faculties; and third, that from the perspective of neuroaesthetics the existence of aesthetic experience as such is potentially up for grabs: but instead of just "having a look," one goes into the lab and tests; the right sort of brain imaging (such as functional magnetic resonance imaging [fMRI]) of subjects enjoying different varieties of art should help determine whether the requisite commonalities obtain. Beyond the depth (i.e., the unavailability to consciousness) of many aspects of ordinary mental life (unconscious aspects of cognition, repressed desires, etc.), the idea is that even a lack of phenomenological similarity across different aesthetic experiences would not by itself imply a lack of subliminal commonality: the hypothesized corticolimbic signature.

Skepticism about the aesthetic approach to the philosophy of art can be handled similarly. Grant that anti-aesthetic art like Duchamp's *Fountain* counts as art, but does not appear to satisfy aesthetic interest or reward aesthetic attention. Still, some people like *Fountain*, and perhaps the deep structure of their appreciation, in concert with a phenomenological sense of similarity (in some cases, though dissimilarity in others) is the same as that of enjoying more standard works. (Such works may unintentionally produce aesthetic experience and thus count as aesthetic despite an artist's possibly anti-aesthetic intentions.) The suggestion is that once again the hypothesis could be tested to find out whether *Fountain really is* anti-aesthetic as Duchamp seems to have intended (though this is itself disputable), bearing in mind that first-person reports are not to be accepted unquestioned or ignored outright, but rather incorporated into a complete picture of the aesthetic situation. If *Fountain* were discovered not to produce aesthetic experience, even in people who do appreciate the work and *as* they do so, that would imply that the appreciation is not of an aesthetic kind, that perhaps Beardsley (1983) was right after all to argue that such works should be seen as curiosities rather than true art objects. Note, though, that *Fountain* might be discovered to produce aesthetic experience in certain people under the right conditions, even perhaps some who firmly believe it could never so move them.

Conclusion

Although the descriptive aspects of art, as described, extend from the armchair all the way to the lab, there is also, undiscussed as yet, some purchase on the value of aesthetic experience, and this will help counter, albeit programmatically here, another objection to the neuroaesthetic approach.

An opponent of neuroaesthetics might object that it is a purely descriptive research program that, as such, fails to account for the *value*, if not the character, of aesthetic experience: the failure of a naturalistic perspective to cross the divide between the agreeable, for which evolutionary explanations are tailor-made, and the truly beautiful, or better, the aesthetically piquant, on which such explanations seemingly must remain silent (Dutton, 2003, p. 703). Such an objection is misguided, and suggests a one-dimensional view of evolution, as if the evolved cortex could not help but find the agreeable (and whatever resembles it) agreeable, the disagreeable (and whatever resembles it) disagreeable, as if it were only things external that matter, ignoring the plausibility that, for all its advantages, cortical evolution is the very cause of many of precisely those psychological conflicts (sometimes *about* the agreeable) for which enjoying art, however transiently, is an effective, and perhaps the preeminent, means of resolution.

References

Baars, B.J. (1999). Art must move: Emotion and the biology of beauty. *Journal of Consciousness Studies, 6*(6-7), 59-61.

Beardsley, M.C. (1981). *Aesthetics: Problems in the philosophy of criticism* (2nd ed.). Indianapolis, IN: Hackett.

Beardsley, M.C. (1983). An aesthetic definition of art. In H. Curtler (Ed.), *What is art?* (pp. 15-29). New York, NY: Haven.

Brown, S., & Dissanayake, E. (2009). The arts are more than aesthetics: Neuroaesthetics as narrow aesthetics. In M. Skov & O. Vartanian (Eds.), *Neuroaesthetics* (pp. 43-57). Amityville, NY: Baywood.

Carroll, N. (2003). Art and mood: Preliminary notes and conjectures. *Monist, 86*, 521-525.

Currie, G. (2003). Aesthetics and cognitive science. In J. Levinson (Ed.), *Oxford handbook of aesthetics* (pp. 706-721). Oxford, UK: Oxford University Press.

Danto, A.C. (1964). The artworld. *Journal of Philosophy, 61*, 571-584.

Danto, A.C. (1981). *The transfiguration of the commonplace.* Cambridge, MA: Harvard University Press.

Davies, S. (1991). *Definitions of art.* Ithaca, NY: Cornell University Press.

Dickie, G. (1964). The myth of the aesthetic attitude. *American Philosophical Quarterly, 1*, 56-65.

Dickie, G. (2000). The institutional theory of art. In N. Carroll (Ed.), *Theories of art today* (pp. 93-108). Madison: University of Wisconsin Press.

Dissanayake, E. (1995). *Homo aestheticus: Where art comes from and why.* Seattle: University of Washington Press.

Dutton, D. (2003). Aesthetics and evolutionary psychology. In J. Levinson (Ed.), *Oxford handbook of aesthetics* (pp. 693-705). Oxford, UK: Oxford University Press.

Gaut, B. (2000). "Art" as a cluster concept. In N. Carroll (Ed.), *Theories of art today* (pp. 25-44). Madison: University of Wisconsin Press.

Gombrich, E.H. (2000). Concerning "The science of art." *Journal of Consciousness Studies, 7*(8-9), 17.

Gregory, R.L. (1999). Object hypotheses in visual perception: David Marr or Cruella de Ville? *Journal of Consciousness Studies, 6* (6-7), 54-56.

Holt, J. (1996). A comprehensivist theory of art. *British Journal of Aesthetics, 36*, 424-431.

Holt, J. (2010). Providing for aesthetic experience. *Reason Papers: A Journal of Interdisciplinary Normative Studies, 32*, 75-91.

Iseminger, G. (2004). *The aesthetic function of art.* Ithaca, NY: Cornell University Press.

Kindy, J. (1999). Of time and beauty. *Journal of Consciousness Studies, 6*(6-7), 61-63.

Koestler, A. (1967). *The ghost in the machine.* London, England: Hutchinson.

Lanier, J. (1999). What information is given by a veil? *Journal of Consciousness Studies, 6*(6-7), 65-68.

Mangan, B. (1999). It don't mean a thing if it ain't got that swing. *Journal of Consciousness Studies, 6*(6-7), 56-58.

Martindale, C. (1999). Peak shift, prototypicality, and aesthetic preference. *Journal of Consciousness Studies, 6*(6-7), 52-54.

Mitter, P. (1999). A short commentary on "The science of art." *Journal of Consciousness Studies, 6*(6-7), 64-65.

Nietzsche, F. (1967). *The birth of tragedy* (W. Kaufman, Trans.). New York, NY: Random House.

Onians, J. (2007). *Neuroarthistory: From Aristotle and Pliny to Baxandall and Zeki.* New Haven, CT: Yale University Press.

Ramachandran, V.S. (2001). Sharpening up "The science of art": An interview with Anthony Freeman. *Journal of Consciousness Studies, 8*(1), 9-29.

Ramachandran, V.S. (2003). *The emerging mind. BBC Reith Lectures, The artful brain* (Lecture 3). Retrieved from http://www.bbc.co.uk/radio4/reith2003/lecture3.shtml.

Ramachandran, V.S., & Hirstein, W. (1999). The science of art: A neurological theory of aesthetic experience. *Journal of Consciousness Studies, 6*(6-7), 15-51.

Richards, I.A., Ogden, C.K., & Wood, J. (1925). *The foundations of aesthetics.* London, England: Harcourt, Brace & World.

Schiller, F. (2004). *On the aesthetic education of man* (R. Snell, Trans.). New York, NY: Dover.

Seeley, W.P. (2006). Naturalizing aesthetics: Art and the cognitive neuroscience of vision. *Journal of Visual Art Practice, 5*, 195-213.

Shusterman, R. (1997). The end of aesthetic experience. *Journal of Aesthetics and Art Criticism, 55*, 29-41.

Simeons, A.T.W. (1961). *Man's presumptuous brain: An evolutionary perspective of psychosomatic disease.* New York, NY: E.P. Dutton.

Skov, M., & Vartanian, O. (Eds.). (2009). *Neuroaesthetics.* Amityville, NY: Baywood.

Stecker, R. (1997). *Artworks: Definition, meaning, value.* University Park: Pennsylvania State University Press.

Tyler, C.W. (1999). Is art lawful? *Science, 285*, 673-674.

Wallen, R. (1999). Response to Ramachandran and Hirstein. *Journal of Consciousness Studies, 6*(6-7), 68-72.

Zeki, S. (1999). *Inner vision: An exploration of art and the brain.* Oxford, UK: Oxford University Press.

Part II

Extensions

7

IS LEONARD COHEN A GOOD SINGER?

When Leonard Cohen accepted the Juno Award for Best Male Vocalist in 1993 for his album *The Future* (the Junos are like Canada's Grammys), he was characteristically self-deprecating, saying that "only in Canada" could he have won such an award. This remark evoked his well-known, ironically self-mocking verdict from "Tower of Song" that his voice is *golden*. While few would contest the substantial quality of Cohen's voice as an artist—that is, his figurative, nonvocal voice— many diehard fans will admit that he's not the *greatest* singer. Yet it seems reasonable to consider as a live question whether he ranks as a good one, and to explore in the process what it means to have artistic merit in such a role as singing. Though some detractors deny that he sings *at all* much less well, many fans would insist, on the contrary, that he's not just a good singer, but so much more.

Does it even make sense to consider seriously the notion that Leonard Cohen is a good singer when it seems pretty clear that he himself doesn't think so? Well, yes. He may not mean it, for one, and even if he does, he could be wrong. It's not just a matter of his opinion, or ours for that matter. Opinions differ widely on many questions, and Cohen's singing is no exception: some critics are too harsh, some fans too forgiving. In matters of taste it is often said "To each their own," and up to a point this is true. Say I like sleeping in, milk in my coffee, and listening to Leonard Cohen—and you don't. That's just fine, and if all people meant by championing or slamming an artist was "I like their work" or "I don't like their work," there would be no issue, no dispute. But that's often not where it stops. Taste tends to assert itself, to vie for dominance. Fandom wants company, and no dissent. Saying that Cohen is a good singer implies not just "I like him" but that *other people* should also so acknowledge him.

Since many fans will be at loggerheads with critics so harsh as to be *anti*-fans, how can we get beyond fandom and anti-fandom to achieve some sort of objectivity? Might we conduct an opinion poll? We could, but mere opinion won't do, as we've seen. Nor is it simply a matter of the numbers, of whether enough people (a majority?) self-identify as "Team Leonard." If it were a matter of popularity, then [*insert current pop phenom here*] would be better than Mozart, but clearly that's not so. Popularity determines neither truth nor quality, and supposing otherwise is fallacious, a reasoning error. Citing the fact that Cohen won a Best Male Vocalist Juno Award doesn't settle the matter either, for we may think—on independent grounds—that someone else should have won instead and that he shouldn't have been in the running. Because we need a real standard, tackling this problem, the problem of taste, will take us deep into philosophy from the shallows of the most egregious internet debates.

Beforehand, though, we should get a few things straight. When we talk about Cohen's singing, we should be clear *which* voice we're talking about: the early baritone (1960s–'70s), or the later bass (1980s–'90s), which are, if both recognizably Cohen, markedly different. The first period extends from *Songs of Leonard Cohen* (1967) through *Recent Songs* (1979), the second roughly from *Various Positions* (1984) to *Ten New Songs* (2001). The he-doesn't-really-sing complaint applies, if anywhere, to *Dear Heather* (2004) and *Old Ideas* (2012), and we should both forgive him this and dismiss the suggestion that such criticism applies in a similar way to his earlier work. The transition is gradual, but the difference is huge. The early voice has more range and urgency, the later greater richness, resonance, a gravitas won not from experience or cigarettes alone. Despite such changes, Cohen's voice admittedly has retained a slightly nasal tone and remained of narrowish range. It's not a generic voice, by any stretch, not generically beautiful either—it's way too distinctive for that.

Cohen's Weight Class

Valid criticisms of Cohen's voice include its limited range and unconventionality, though more from a pop music than folk perspective. He's no Sinatra or Callas, to be sure, but it would be woefully unfair to set the bar that high. Good does not imply keeping pace with the great. It also would be unfair of us to judge Frank Sinatra by the standards of opera, or Maria Callas by those of jazz or pop music. Each is a great singer in their own domain or "weight class," and so too, I suggest, should we judge Leonard Cohen. In evaluating Cohen's voice, we should consider his weight class, which straddles the divide between folk and popular music. With one foot in each genre, Cohen weighs in—as we knew he would—as a singer-songwriter (for slightly different emphasis, songwriter-singer). Just as we "forgive" Sinatra for not writing songs, or Cole Porter for not being a singer, so too should we "forgive" singer-songwriters for lacking Sinatra's voice or Porter's writing chops. Being *good enough* at both is pretty impressive.

Perhaps, then, the question "Is Leonard Cohen a good singer?" isn't quite right. Maybe the better question, apropos of his Juno Award, would be "Is Cohen a good *vocalist*?" or, even better, vocal *stylist*. One strong influence on Cohen's musical style is often acknowledged to be the French *chanson* as exemplified by such artists as Jacques Brel, where, as David Boucher observes in *Dylan and Cohen*, "the aesthetic sound of the voice determines the excellence of the work; for the *chansonnier*, it is style that matters and not perfect pitch or polished performance" (p. 137). Now the idea *isn't* that Cohen isn't a bad singer because he's not really trying to be a good one. Rather, knocking his voice for being in a particular musical style or tradition will count less as criticism of Cohen himself and more as a complaint, whether just or prejudicial, about the entire tradition. Still, pigeonholing Cohen as a *chansonnier* seems to sell both him and his voice short. Cohen's distinctive, personal vocal style inherits from yet transcends folk, blues, country, pop—various traditions.

No discussion of Cohen's weight class would be complete without ranking him vocally relative to other singer-songwriters. We should note (along with David Hume) that this isn't mere opining, either, as such ranking can be an entirely objective matter where any dissent wouldn't be taken too seriously (pp. 40–41), as in the case of someone's hyperfandom moving them to proclaim [*insert current action movie star*] a better actor than Laurence Olivier. Among other singer-songwriters, it seems fair to see Cohen somewhere in the middle of the vocal quality spectrum, ranking below a Paul Simon but above a Bob Dylan; for a Canadian trifecta, let's substitute Gordon Lightfoot above and Neil Young below. Remember that as singer-songwriters, those tending toward the bottom of the vocal spectrum still have mediocre voices, which by implication means those like Cohen above are in the better-than-mediocre category: in other words, good.

Consider now what I'd like to call the great singer-songwriter argument, which goes something like this. Because being a singer-songwriter depends on two very different skill sets, such status implies a basic level of competence in both domains. In other words, you can't even *be* a singer-songwriter without being dually capable of writing songs as well as singing them. By extension, how highly one rates as a singer-songwriter has implications for singing and songwriting ability. An excellent singer might be a lousy singer-songwriter, but just as a great hunter-gatherer has to be a pretty good hunter *and* a pretty good gatherer—though not necessarily supreme in either—so too must a *great* singer-songwriter be, at the very least, a pretty good singer, even if, as with Cohen, the songwriting appears superior to the singing and allows us to forgive imperfections in the latter. In a nutshell, then, the argument is that because Cohen is a *great* singer-songwriter, he also, by implication, counts as at least a decent singer. Although Bob Dylan is unquestionably a great songwriter, one could argue, by contrast, that his voice limits his singer-songwriter rank to something short of great, the upper echelons of good.

Style Prejudice

When we consider the role of experts in guiding our aesthetic choices, we naturally think of popular types of criticism: movie critics, food critics, literary critics, music critics. Although today's internet culture fosters what we may kindly call "democratic" approaches to criticism, where everyone's keen to assert their own taste alone, and it's always open season on anyone and anything, most of us still incline toward respect for certain expert critics. Good critics are able to discern, better than others, the qualities that make art—whether we're talking about a film, a singer, what have you—good, or worthy of attention. Being in a position to make those aesthetic judgments requires perceiving and responding to the relevant features of a variety of different examples, and doing so impartially (or, as David Hume put it, having a "strong sense, united to delicate sentiment, improved by practice, perfected by comparison, and cleared of all prejudice," p. 44).

That we should be "cleared of all prejudice" is something we should remind about 95 percent of all internet commentators. We sometimes associate such critical harshness, whether we find it on the internet or elsewhere, with justified opinion if not expertise. But such harshness can often conceal underlying prejudice. Take the following pre-internet pronouncement from critic Juan Rodriguez: "Although Cohen may have a private affinity for the vitality, ease and emotive qualities of pop music at its best . . . this does not automatically provide him with the talent to sing. Cohen plainly cannot sing. His voice is dull and monotonous and has little range" (p. 67). This reads like the sentence of a pretty uncompromising judge, who would be similarly tough assessing others and whose apparently principled stance commands our respect. However, the critic's evaluation unfolds rather surprisingly: "Bob Dylan, on the other hand, does know how to sing and he makes his own rough and unsweet voice an attribute, not a liability. Unfortunately, Cohen has been able to do nothing with his voice and this fact turns up in his melodies, which are slow, deadeningly similar, and wholly uninspiring." Ouch; the sting of it isn't the point, though. Rather, with this unexpected turn the critic has lost, maybe not all, but most of us. Whatever we might think of the relative merits of the two voices, they're not *that* different in terms of aesthetic judgment, not night-and-day different.

This passage also illustrates a significant and usually unacknowledged source of many negative impressions of Cohen as a singer: *style prejudice*. A lot of people simply don't like his style, any part of it, the way Cohen dresses, his poet-polished lyrics, his aesthetic sensibility, the ironic tone and dark, existential mood of many of his songs. Notice how the critic above linked what he dislikes about Cohen's voice with his dislike of the music itself, suggesting that melodic "disappointment" somehow reveals vocal inadequacy. Some don't like the romanticism, others the realism, others still the combination. To gloss any of these dislikes as "vocal inadequacy" is simply what philosophers call a category-mistake: a misattribution error. People who dismiss his singing are sometimes no more forgiving of more generically approved singers' covers (as with Jennifer Warnes's *Famous Blue Raincoat* tribute album), which indicates the issue isn't really Cohen's singing so much as the songs themselves. Preferring a cover to a Cohen original might also, but also might not, betray a style prejudice.

A similar style and content prejudice can be seen in attitudes toward the music of Tom Waits, whose voice is also unconventional and whose songs, next to Cohen's, are comparably nostalgic, gloomy, and depressing. There's nothing wrong with preferring, as I confess I do, the more conventional, smoother voice of Waits's early *The Heart of Saturday Night* (1974) to the roughed up vocals of his more experimental later work, but to transmute this preference into a negative *verdict* is again simply a style prejudice. Similarly, many who dismiss the folk baritone of the early Cohen probably haven't given his later pop bass a real chance, and those who deny that Cohen sings at all likely haven't really considered such early performances as "Stories of the Street" or "Sing Another Song, Boys."

The *Je Ne Sais Quoi*

Although some take to Cohen's voice right away and others never do, still others come around after repeated or prolonged exposure. For some, in other words, Leonard Cohen is an acquired taste. To this extent, the pleasures of listening to Cohen are not unlike those derived from some alcoholic beverages, certain foods, and smoking, which typically require overcoming an initial negative reaction. Most people find their first exposure to the taste of beer, the texture of sushi, and inhaling smoke to be somewhere on the continuum between rather offputting and outright revolting. I suspect that Cohen himself would not find the comparisons insulting. Some people never get over their initial negative reactions, and that's fine. But the fans and critics who have managed to cross over, or who haven't had to, are able to enjoy whole spheres of experience, of pleasure, to which the rest of the world remains closed. To transpose a local beer ad into Cohen fandom terms, those who like him like him *a lot*.

To appreciate the importance of this point, that for many Cohen is an acquired taste, we should remind ourselves that, for Hume, part of being a good critic is sensitively discerning the relevant qualities, the aesthetic character, of the thing being judged. To the extent that Cohen is an acquired taste, his detractors might never be in a position to perceive the qualities that many fans and music critics enjoy. It's not that they *dislike* what the likers like, but rather that they've not managed to overcome their natural resistance to even experiencing, much less considering, what fans appreciate. As connoisseurs of beer or wine are able to discern qualities that dislikers simply can't, so too might the same be said for true Leonard Cohen aficionados.

What fans and many critics experience in Cohen, to the extent that this can be described at all, is a distinctive voice singing unique songs with genuinely poetic lyrics and that express a significant artistic vision. The distinctiveness of the singing matches the personal quality of the lyrics, which unlike almost all other folk or pop songs do more than gesture at poetry. Cohen's lyrics don't just gesture, they achieve, they *are*. Most generic voices are less distinctive and less distinct in expressing lyrics that seldom merit the emphasis of Cohenesque enunciation. Where some listeners might resent that Cohen's singing style betrays such an extraordinarily exacting concern with language, a loving exactitude, this care is part of what fans appreciate in his voice along with the sense of intimacy it suggests and explores with the listener. It's a voice rich with the attempt to share with the listener something both important and well-turned. Cohen's voice suits its poetic material.

As many critics, not just fans, see it, Cohen's voice has a mysterious, enigmatic quality, an undeniable *je ne sais quoi*. Critics observe in the DVD *Leonard Cohen: Under Review* that his voice has an "immense personal charm. You want to engage him when you hear his voice coming out of the speakers" (Robert Christgau). "It has a very hypnotic quality" (Anthony DeCurtis). But figuring out exactly why isn't so easy: "Is it the quality of his voice? Is it the way he dramatizes himself? I think that these things are very mysterious" (Christgau). Part of the answer might be found in a thought-provoking comment by Ronee Blakley, who also sang backup on *Death of a Ladies' Man* (1977):

> Leonard has in his voice a slight trembling from time to time which is extremely vulnerable and real and present and there. It's at the front of his head, though it almost has a rumbling sound, a biblical sound at times. It can also sound very sensitive and charming and this sound that he has in addition to the rabbinical quality... is almost what in Christian music would be called *bel canto* or *cantus firmus*: the kind that monks would sing...

This comment suggests to my mind two very provocative things about Cohen's voice: first, that it succeeds in part by somehow tapping into our musical subconscious; and second, that it works not necessarily despite but also oddly *because of* its particular imperfections. A better voice just wouldn't be *Leonard Cohen's*. Would it make sense to wish him better endowed? I really don't think so. It seems we'd be missing the point.

99

No Accounting?

As I write this I glance at a ticket stub propped up against my laptop: Section 37, Row J, Seat 2, not just a ticket, *my* ticket, for the Leonard Cohen concert at the Halifax Metro Centre, April 13, 2013. It reads "On stage promptly at 8 pm," which he was, and he played for three and a quarter hours. It was the second time I'd seen him live, the first also in Halifax in 2008 at a venue—and so he recalled in the 2013 concert—called the Cohn auditorium. Though I'd been a fan for very many years, I never thought I'd be fortunate enough to get to see him live, much less twice. The aura hasn't faded yet. But it gives me pause, this highly personal experience, shared with Megan (Seat 1) and thousands of others: communication as communion. It was, and remains, perhaps a perfect example of how art can—somehow, seemingly—personalize the universal, universalize the personal. Can I convey what it meant to me? Not exactly, though I can gesture at it. Could I convince someone who didn't like it that they should have? Probably not. "It's good but I don't like it" is no paradox. Good standards limit judgment without compelling taste.

This might remind you of the old chestnut, "There's no accounting for taste," a sensible but still ambiguous adage. It might mean that you can't explain why someone has the particular likes or dislikes they do, or that there's ultimately no justification for taste "beyond itself"— as the bromide goes, it is what it is. Hume, on the other hand, thought that there *is* accounting for taste, in terms of human nature, which he saw as uniform. That uniformity explains why there can be lasting consensus on great artists like Homer (p. 42). When there are aesthetic disputes, Hume thought, that's because some of the disputants lack true expertise, missing the right sensitivities or being subject to forgivable age- or culture-specific tendencies. In some cases, too, there will be unavoidable idiosyncrasies of personal taste that don't really touch on aesthetic disputes. Suppose, for instance, when it comes to Cohen, I prefer his realism, you his romanticism, though we agree that he's a great artist.

Can we confidently say that Hume-approved experts will agree that Leonard Cohen is a good singer? Not necessarily, though I've given some reason to suppose they may. It's actually pretty tough to figure out who, if anyone, the Hume-approved critics are. Given how vehement the disputes among critics, all of whom have some claim to objectivity, often get, and how rare consensus among them really is except in—fittingly—exceptional cases, perhaps human nature and aesthetic judgment aren't uniform but varied, pluralistic. Good critics then would be seen in terms of sub-universal but legit spheres of appropriate influence. But does this not just dissolve into utter subjectivity, an aesthetic of idiosyncrasy? Perhaps my enjoyment of Leonard Cohen's singing voice is mere preference after all.

Is that all there is? Maybe, and I'll tell you why. In my late teens I was depressive to the point of suicidal. My parents were naturally concerned, more so as the usual ways of addressing the problem proved ineffective. The depression and I were stubborn, lonely and painful as it got. My father did something totally counterintuitive but ultimately inspired: he bought me *The Best of Leonard Cohen* (1975) on cassette. Who would think to give their suicidal son "music to slit your wrists to"? And yet, as I listened, I resonated with the music, with Cohen's voice, all of it, with such immediacy, such intensity, it was so resolutive—it saved my life. How could that not cloud, in the best possible way, my judgment, biasing me toward the one voice that reached me through the darkness?

References

Boucher, David. 2004. *Dylan and Cohen: Poets of Rock and Roll.* New York: Continuum.

Hume, David. 2002. Of the Standard of Taste. In *The Nature of Art: An Anthology*, edited by Thomas E. Wartenberg, 39-47. Orlando: Harcourt.

Leonard Cohen: Under Review 1934-1977. 2007. DVD. New Malden: Chrome Dreams.

Rodriguez, Juan. 1976. Poet's Progress—To Sainthood and Back. In *Leonard Cohen: The Artist and His Critics*, edited by Michael Gnarowski, 63-68. Toronto: McGraw-Hill Ryerson.

8 WOODY ON AESTHETIC APPRECIATION

Woody Allen is not a philosopher. He'd be the first to admit it. Much of his work does, however, have philosophical significance. This is hardly surprising if one observes that while good philosophy tends to be aesthetically piquant, good art likewise tends to be philosophically insightful. Now Woody might reject the label *artist*. There are certainly clues to this effect, possibly ironic, possibly sincere. The label might, at the very least, cause him some discomfort. But as we already know, the label is appropriate, and not just by common standards. Woody is, if nothing else, an entertainer, and he entertains, as a matter of fact, "on a very high level," bringing "a great sense of excitement, stimulation, and fulfillment to people who are sensitive and cultivated."[1] This, by his own standards, makes him not only an artist, but a very good one.

The philosophical relevance of many Woody Allen films is most evident in the exploration of such topics as the meaning of life, existential angst, and moral crisis. Other matters of concern are addressed more subtly, often humorously. The effect is twofold. While the humor distracts us from the matter at hand, obscuring its own foundations, its own implicit assumptions, it also lends credence to those assumptions. It's not that what's funny is true. There are different ways of making people laugh. Rather, Woody's humor is funny in such a way that it vindicates itself as insightful, although again, the matter and insight are often easy enough to miss.

Case in point: the nature of aesthetic appreciation. I will present a straightforward but, I think, insightful view of aesthetic appreciation

---

[1]Stig Björkman, ed., *Woody Allen on Woody Allen* (New York: Grove Press, 1993), p. 103.

that emerges from Woody Allen's work, chiefly, but not exclusively, his films, and among them chiefly, but not exclusively, *Manhattan*, *Hannah and Her Sisters*, and *Crimes and Misdemeanors*. Why these three? Well, I'm a Woody fan, and these are my all-time favorites. They also happen to contain a high concentration of germane source material. By way of support, other works in the Woody *oeuvre* will be used. At the same time, however, I do not pretend that this is an exhaustive work of scholarship. My primary interest is in the *gestalt*, and in such details from the *oeuvre* as are sufficient to suggest it. Not only will I ignore much of Woody's work, I will also, for the most part, ignore the man himself. With all due respect, it is the significance of the work that interests me, not whether, or to what extent, the man himself intended the work to have such significance. After all, Woody would probably sell himself short.

In a nutshell, my view is that aesthetic appreciation involves a blending of both intellectual and emotional responses. Both are necessary, but neither is sufficient. Over-intellectualization inhibits, or serves as a sham substitute for, the emotional response involved in genuine appreciation, yielding a knowledgeable but ultimately superficial approach to art. By the same token, excessive emotionality inhibits, or serves as a sham substitute for, the requisite intellectual ingredient, yielding a heartfelt but ultimately indiscriminate approach to art. In genuine appreciation, there is a balance between the two kinds of response. Neither predominates, and the usual conflict between the two is resolved. What such "resolution" means deserves to be explored, and the implications of this view for the way we understand art are important.

Word to the wise: In writing this, I am *not* over-intellectualizing my aesthetic appreciation of Woody's work. That is another matter, falling within another domain. This is an exercise, not in aesthetic appreciation, but in philosophical extrusion. In the spirit of the view to follow, I would not presume to substitute the latter for the former, although the latter may abet the former in interesting ways.

A Marvelous Negative Capability

Much contemporary art is baffling. The art world is permeated with what Arthur Danto calls an "atmosphere of theory," ignorance of which leaves many artworks difficult if not impossible to grasp.[2] It seems that if one is to appreciate theory-driven work, one needs to be conversant with the relevant theory. To some extent this may be true. If an artist's intentions are theoretically couched or sensitive, and if one seeks to understand art in terms of what the artist intended, then such an approach makes perfect sense. It also makes sense if one seeks to interpret art according to established critical procedures, irrespective of whether they pay heed to the artist's intentions. Where theory is needed, let theory reign.

But these are not the only legitimate interests one may have in approaching art. One may, and often should, approach art for the sake of one's own aesthetic pleasure. Even if such gratification falls short of what some authority deems "understanding," it does not fall short of, but rather *constitutes*, genuine appreciation. Let Woody's humor guide us. Woody is arguably at his funniest when he lampoons over-intellectualized approaches to art. Inhaling the "atmosphere of theory" too deeply is seen as inhibiting genuine appreciation, serving as a sham substitute for it, and worse, delegitimating the genuine appreciation of others. Such a stance is overly critical, and at the same time, overly generous. It's pedantic, jargonized, designed to impress, which leads, in some cases, to outright contradiction, which is a theoretical defeater if anything is.

Let's take some examples. Sally (Judy Davis) in *Husbands and Wives* illustrates how over-intellectualization can make one hyper-critical, inhibiting one's appreciation, and delegitimating that of others. Notice how this plays out with Michael (Liam Neeson) in their discussion of Mahler's *Ninth*:

Michael: That music was fantastic.
Sally: I usually hate Mahler, but it was good. The last
            movement was too long. I think he should have
            cut it down. The second movement was good.
            Well, it *began* well. Then it gets sentimental,
            don't you think?[3]

She goes on, in hyper-critical mode, to berate his driving, her own décor, and the alfredo sauce at dinner. The last is an oh-so-subtle echo of Woody's short "Fabrizio's: Criticism and Response."[4]

---

[2]See Arthur Danto, *The Transfiguration of the Commonplace* (Cambridge: Harvard University Press, 1981), p. 135.

[3]*Husbands and Wives* (1992).

[4]*Side Effects* (1981).

Hyper-criticality is also evident in the famous Marshall McLuhan scene in *Annie Hall*. Before the McLuhanese of "hot" and "cool" media is bandied about, much to the irritation of Alvy (Woody), the Professor (Russell Horton), standing behind him in line, gives a mini seminar on Fellini, also to Alvy's great irritation:

> Professor: We saw the Fellini film last Tuesday. It is *not* one of his best. It lacks a cohesive structure, you know? You get the feeling that he's not absolutely sure what it is he wants to *say*. Of course, I've always felt that he was essentially a—a *technical* film-maker. Granted, *La Strada* was a great film, great in its use of negative imagery more than anything else. But that simple, cohesive core... Like all that *Juliet of the Spirits* or *Satyricon*, I found it incredibly *indulgent*, you know? He really is. He's one of the most *indulgent* film-makers. He really is.[5]

One can also see, here, shades of jargonization—yes, I intend the irony—not to mention outright contradiction. To impress his listener, obviously, the professor dismisses Fellini first as a merely technical film-maker, then as a supremely indulgent one. In *Hannah and Her Sisters*, a similar phenomenon is at work when David (Sam Waterston) shows Holly (Dianne Wiest) and April (Carrie Fisher) one of his buildings:

> David: The design's deliberately non-contextual, but I wanted to keep the atmosphere of the street, you know, and in the proportions, and in the material, that's—that's unpolished red granite.
> April: It has an organic quality, you know? It's almost—almost—uh—entirely wholly interdependent, if you know what I mean. I can't put it into words. The important thing is that it—it *breathes*.[6]

April jargonizes, putting into vague terms what she says can't be put in any terms, while David's idea of non-contextual architecture involves

---

[5] *Annie Hall* (1977).
[6] *Hannah and Her Sisters* (1986).

paying attention to the atmosphere, proportions, and material of the surrounding buildings.

A different but related case is Lester (Alan Alda) in *Crimes and Misdemeanors*. His language, in talking about art, is not pedantic or self-contradictory, nor is it hyper-critical, at least not explicitly. He is, however, somewhat dismissive. Of Chekov stories he says, off the cuff, "The guy wrote a *million* of them." When Emily Dickinson comes up in conversation over drinks, Halley (Mia Farrow) begins quoting from "The Chariot," and the ensuing dynamic between her, Cliff (Woody), and Lester is quite telling:

Halley:	"Because I could not stop for death—"
Cliff:	"—He kindly stopped for me." The word *kindly*, right?[7]

It's out of appreciation that Halley begins the quotation, and it's a shared appreciation that prompts Cliff to continue, stressing the adverb that makes the couplet work. Lester ignores this, and continues to quote the stanza in its entirety, as if rote memorization is what really counts. By implication, appreciating the way words are used in the poem—appreciating the poem itself—is dismissed as a side-issue, or worse, a non-issue.

The character that perhaps best exhibits over-intellectualization is Mary (Diane Keaton) in *Manhattan*. Witness the variety of symptoms in the following exchange with Isaac (Woody):

Isaac:	The photographs downstairs—great, absolutely great. Did you like it?
Mary:	No. I felt it was very derivative. To me it looked like it was straight out of Diane Arbus, but it had none of the wit.
Isaac:	Well, we didn't like it as much as we liked the plexiglass sculpture, that I will admit.
Mary:	Really. You liked the plexiglass?
Isaac:	You didn't like the plexiglass sculpture either?
Mary:	Interesting. No, um, uh-uh.
Isaac:	It was a hell of a lot better than that steel cube. Did you see the steel cube?
Mary:	Now that was brilliant to me, absolutely brilliant.

---

[7] *Crimes and Misdemeanors* (1989).

Isaac:	The steel cube was brilliant?
Mary:	Yes. To me it was very textural, you know what I mean? It was perfectly integrated, and it had a marvelous kind of negative capability. The rest of the stuff downstairs was bullshit.[8]

Isaac dismisses this as "pseudo-intellectual garbage," which perhaps it is, although the underlying problem, again, is that art is being approached in an overly rational fashion. Later, in reference to a piece of sculpture, Isaac pokes fun at this attitude:

Isaac:	This I think has a—a kind of wonderful *otherness* to it, you know? It's kind of got a marvelous *negative capability*, a kind of wonderful *energy*, don't you think?[9]

Mary's hyper-criticality is also exhibited in her role as co-founder of the Academy of the Over-Rated, the ironic counterpoint of which is that, while she's happy to berate Mahler, Fitzgerald, van Gogh, and Bergman, she insists that many of her friends deserve the title of genius, to say nothing of her ex-husband Jeremiah (Wallace Shawn).

I Love Songs About Extra-Terrestrial Life, Don't You?

Just as over-intellectualizing art is a problem, so too is *under*-intellectualizing it. In such cases, the culprit is excessive emotionality, which inhibits, or serves as a sham substitute for, the intellectual component of genuine appreciation. The result here is a heartfelt but ultimately indiscriminate approach to art, as when Holly takes Mickey (Woody) to a rock concert in *Hannah and Her Sisters*:

Holly:	I love songs about extra-terrestrial life, don't you?
Mickey:	Not when they're sung by extra-terrestrials.[10]

Similarly, notice what happens in the exchange between Frederick (Max von Sydow) the artist and Dusty (Daniel Stern) the rock star:

---

[8] *Manhattan* (1979).
[9] *Ibid.*
[10] *Hannah and Her Sisters* (1986).

Dusty:	I got an Andy Warhol, and I got a Frank Stella too. Oh, it's very beautiful, *big*, *weird*. If you stare at that Stella too long, the colors just seem to float. It's—kind of weird....
Frederick:	Do you appreciate drawings?
Dusty:	Yeah. Oh, hey, wow. She's beautiful. But, uh, I really need something—I'm looking for something *big*.... I got a lot of wall space there....
Frederick:	I—*don't*—sell my work by the yard.[11]

The indiscriminate emotionality of Holly is complemented, here, by Dusty's confusion. In Frederick's drawings, he mistakes the beauty of the woman depicted for the beauty of the depiction. (Think of Magritte's infamous *Çeci n'est pas une pipe*.) More amusingly, his criterion as "art collector" is not the beauty, piquancy, or value of a piece, but rather, of all things, its *size*, and its ability to blend in with his sofa—er, sorry—his ottoman.

Other characters in Woody's films exhibit similar tendencies, but the examples above are, to my mind, the most memorable. Still, one may wonder whether there are other sorts of evidence that, on the Allenesque view, aesthetic appreciation involves a significant intellectual ingredient. There are, one of which comes from the man himself, specifically, Woody's definition of art as "entertainment for intellectuals."[12] I have to admit, this is a pretty good definition. Few philosophers could do better. The point, though, is that if this is what art is conceived to be, then aesthetic appreciation must be likewise conceived as involving a certain intellectual sensitivity, cultivation, and, in the moment, engagement. Otherwise it wouldn't be *for* intellectuals.

The Brain Is My Second Favorite Organ

It's time now to put the pieces together. Aesthetic appreciation involves both the intellect and the emotions. It's not overly intellectual, in the sense that one lacks the requisite emotionality. Nor is it overly emotional, in the sense that one lacks intellectual refinement and discrimination. The two are rather in balance. What would otherwise be base pleasure is distinctively elevated, and what would otherwise be detached abstraction is distinctively grounded. Quality art affects us

---

[11] *Ibid.*
[12] Björkman (1993), p. 103.

in both ways, moving us in thought as well as in feeling. A Lester-like way of putting this is to say that Piquancy = Profundity + Poignancy.

In art, profundity engages the intellect, poignancy the emotions, and the experience as a whole is aesthetically piquant. Of course, one can encounter art without being moved to thought or feeling, but in such cases, one fails to appreciate it, or one has a merely intellectual or merely emotional appreciation, and while such appreciation is of aesthetic objects, neither is genuinely aesthetic.

What is the value of such experiences? Woody gives us a clue. In *Manhattan*, artworks and artists dominate Isaac's list of what makes life worth living: "the second movement of the *'Jupiter' Symphony*, Louis Armstrong's recording of 'Potato Head Blues,' Swedish movies [read: 'the films of Ingmar Bergman'], naturally, *Sentimental Education* by Flaubert, Marlon Brando, Frank Sinatra," and of course, "those incredible apples and pears by Cézanne."[13]

Fair enough. But why should experiencing such things *aesthetically* be so crucially important? Again, Woody gives us a clue. The characters he portrays are almost invariably in *conflict*—between what they want to do and think they ought to do, between their sense of justice and the recognition of injustice, between their desires and the knowledge that many of them can't be satisfied, and so on. These, if you notice, are conflicts between intellect and emotion. Reason and passion are at odds, and their being at odds is typical of mental life, all too typical.[14] As Cliff puts it: "My heart says one thing, my head says something else. It's very difficult to get your heart and your head together in life."[15] One needs relief from such conflict, and one finds relief in art.

To appreciate art, to experience it aesthetically, amounts to a *resolution* of conflict between intellect and emotion.[16] Although such resolution is often, and perhaps characteristically, pleasurable, it need not have a sedative, calming effect, because aesthetic experience, so conceived, is not a quelling of the faculties, as in sleep, but a coherent engagement of both. Indeed, aesthetic experience is often quite

---

[13] *Manhattan* (1979).

[14] See A.T.W. Simeons, *Man's Presumptuous Brain* (New York: E.P. Dutton, 1961), especially pp. 31-59.

[15] *Crimes and Misdemeanors* (1989).

[16] In some respects, this is rooted in I.A. Richards, *Principles of Literary Criticism* (London: Routledge, 1925), which is cited with approval in Monroe Beardsley, *Aesthetics* (New York: Harcourt, Brace, 1958), pp. 573-74, and echoed in my "A Comprehensivist Theory of Art," *British Journal of Aesthetics* 36 (1996), pp. 427-28.

exciting, inspiring thought and action in a way which, arguably, the conflicted mind simply can't equal.

It is a virtue of this view that it provides such a straightforward account of the value of aesthetic experience. Another virtue is this. Some philosophers are skeptics about aesthetic experience.[17] That is, they doubt that there is anything distinctive about it, that there is anything that all, and only, such experiences share. While the motives for such skepticism vary, the best justification for it seems to be that art can and often does have a huge variety of psychological effects.[18] First, some aesthetic experiences appear to be not so much cognitive as *sensuous*. Think, for instance, of appreciating instrumental music, an appreciation which, plausibly enough, seems more purely experiential, more basely pleasurable, than a marriage of intellect and emotion. Even in the cognitive realm, intellectual and emotional content varies widely. What could my laughter at a comedy and my tears at a tragedy possibly have in common? More precisely (if still somewhat simplistically), suppose a tragedy moves me to sad thoughts of terrible fate, while a comedy induces happy thoughts of felicitous coincidence. What could these responses have in common?

Let's tackle these in turn. First, it's not at all obvious that purely sensuous experiences are genuinely aesthetic. As with purely intellectual or purely emotional responses to art, a purely sensuous response may be *of* an aesthetic object without itself being aesthetic in character. Aesthetic pleasure is almost undeniably unlike the sort of base pleasure one enjoys in other domains (although undoubtedly these pleasures may be invested with aesthetic significance). It *feels* different. And even if it didn't, the pleasure of aesthetic experience may simply distract us—as pleasure often does—from distinct, and introspectable, cognitive ingredients. When we find a piece of music piquant, it moves us, stirring up emotions, dredging up thoughts. Where cognitive elements can't be introspected, this suggests that, as the source of aesthetic pleasure, they are not absent but *deep*, emotions one knows not what, an implicit cognitive grasp of the piece's melodic patterns, harmonic structures, and so on. That aesthetic pleasure is so often sought, yet comparatively difficult to come by, suggests that it is altogether different in kind from its purely sensuous counterpart.

This leaves us with the problem of cognitive variance, that is, the

---

[17]For instance, George Dickie, "The Myth of the Aesthetic Attitude," *American Philosophical Quarterly* 1 (1964), pp. 56-65.

[18]Stephen Davies, *Definitions of Art* (Ithaca: Cornell University Press, 1991), pp. 59-60.

problem of how two different experiences could count as aesthetic when they share neither intellectual nor emotional content. Suppose that my emotional response to a tragedy is sadness, while my emotional response to a comedy is happiness; and where the tragedy suggests the thought that even heroes are doomed, that life is most grave indeed, the comedy suggests that even fools will prosper, that life is anything but serious. In each case I am responding to an artwork, but—and this is the key question—in what sense is it plausible to say that the two experiences have the *same* aesthetic character? After all, the sadness of my tragedy-response is contrary to the happiness of my comedy-response. My respective thoughts are likewise incompatible. But on the Allenesque view, it's the balance that matters, reason and passion united, not the particular intellectual or emotional content of the experience. My sad tragic thoughts exhibit this harmony. My happy comic thoughts do too. In the first case, my sadness is not in conflict, but rather coheres, with the tragic thought, and as such does not move me to seek means of alleviation. Likewise, my happiness coheres *in the same way* with my intellectual response to the comedy. The two responses, again, are in concert, mutually supportive. Variety notwithstanding, then, there is something that all, and only, aesthetic experiences share. They're *resolutive*.[19] Thus does Woody score, in my view, a hit, a very palpable hit.

Don't Speak

Ludwig Wittgenstein concludes his famous *Tractatus* with: "Whereof one cannot speak, thereof one must be silent."[20] As Wittgenstein pictures it, we can't speak of matters in the realm of value, which includes, of course, the aesthetic. The aesthetic is one of those things that can be *shown*, and so, in a sense, shared. But the aesthetic can't be captured in language. It can't be so reduced. The Allenesque view is similar. Notice the dynamic of shared appreciation between Isaac and Tracy (Mariel Hemingway) in *Manhattan*, between Elliot (Michael Caine) and Lee (Barbara Hershey) in *Hannah and Her Sisters*, between Cliff and Halley in *Crimes and Misdemeanors*. In character, Woody

---

[19] A term from Holt (1996), pp. 427-28 meaning "exhibits, and consists in, resolution" in the special sense of 'resolution' intended. The usual adjectival forms 'resolved', 'resolving', and the like, did not seem apt.

[20] Ludwig Wittgenstein, *Tractatus Logico-Philosophicus* (New York: Harcourt, Brace, 1933), Proposition 7.

almost invariably expresses aesthetic approbation in the form of simple, positive statements: "Great," "Terrific," "Fantastic," "Wonderful," and so on. Woody's riff on Wittgenstein, then, is: "Whereof one cannot speak, thereof one must say little." To say more than a little, it seems, is not only to miss the point, it is to over-intellectualize art and thereby preclude genuine appreciation of it.

It's here that Woody and I part ways, and here's why. An overly intellectual or emotional approach to art precludes genuine appreciation, yes. But what determines the excessiveness of either is that it is "all out of proportion" to, and thus has the danger of inhibiting, the other. But proportionality is relative. What would otherwise be an excess of thought can be matched by what would otherwise be an excess of feeling, and slight excesses of one, deliberate or otherwise, in the privacy of thought or in discussion with others, may augment the other into a higher, more insightful, more moving resolution. If genuine appreciation is a seesaw balance between intellect and emotion, this does not by itself determine how low, or high, the fulcrum should be set.[21]

[21]My thanks to Mark Conard, Aeon Skoble, and Elana Geller for comments on an earlier draft.

9   TERMINATOR-FEAR AND THE PARADOX OF FICTION

POSSIBLE RESPONSE[S]:

> YES/NO
> OR WHAT?
> GO AWAY
> PLEASE COME BACK LATER
> . . .

—The Terminator's language processor (heads-up display)

Some of the most vividly unnerving scenes in *The Terminator* (James Cameron, 1984) are those that present the Terminator's point of view, giving us a sense of what it would be like to be the Terminator, to see the world as it does, to have not only artificial intelligence but also, more disturbingly, artificial consciousness. The judicious use of the subjective camera is an especially effective technique when appropriately modified to evoke alien perspectives, those radically unlike our own. The Terminator's visual field is infrared, with heads-up displays for attentional shift and focus, information processing of different kinds, decision-making menus, and action-guiding schematics. Although in some sense we can never know what it is like to be a creature whose consciousness is radically different from our own, *The Terminator* gives us the imaginative wherewithal to grasp what an artificial consciousness might be like, more vividly and effectively perhaps than other AI-heavy films, such as *2001: A Space Odyssey* (Stanley Kubrick, 1968) and *Blade Runner* (Ridley Scott, 1982), which neglect or marginalize the first-"person" perspective on artificial consciousness, especially as it is likely to be something radically unlike our own.[1]

The basic premise of *The Terminator* is as follows: from a post-apocalyptic future in which humans are on the brink of winning a long-standing war with rogue machines, a Terminator (Arnold Schwarzenegger) is sent back in time to kill Sarah Connor (Linda Hamilton) before the birth of her son John, the leader of the human revolt and sine qua non of its success; to protect his mother and save himself from "retroactive abortion," John sends back his brother in arms and not-yet father, Kyle Reese (Michael Biehn).[2]

Time travel and artificial intelligence, not to mention a healthy (or unhealthy) dose of technophobia and technophilia, are science fiction staples, and *The Terminator* blends them well in its cinematic style (viz. the nightclub aesthetic of Tech Noir). The received wisdom is that both artificial intelligence and time travel are possible, the latter at least theoretically, and though awareness of this should inform our reactions to science fiction scenarios, the more central issue is the emotional reactions themselves.[3] I suggest that we find the Terminator's alien, in many ways superior, artificial consciousness to be at least as unsettling as the physical threat the Terminator poses. This is brought home more than anything else by the first-"person" Terminator perspective shots. When the Terminator chases Sarah and Reese down a dark alley, its unimpeded infrared visual display calls up a crosshair scope to track them, focusing the Terminator's visual attention and mortal intention alike. At the police station shoot 'em up, its vision unimpaired in the blackout, the Terminator perceives and acts in what appears to be slow motion. When it digitizes and stores information, such as the address of Sarah's mother's cabin, we know that the information will not be forgotten. When it climbs into the cab of an

---

[1] Thomas Nagel, "What Is It Like To Be a Bat?" *Philosophical Review* 83 (1974): 435-50.

[2] The screenplay was written by James Cameron and Gale Anne Hurd, with additional dialogue by William Wisher, Jr. The works of Harlan Ellison are acknowledged at the end of the film, although not specifically Ellison's "Soldier" and "Demon with a Glass Hand," teleplays for the original *Outer Limits* TV series.

[3] If time travel is possible, then it must be possible to affect the past. But being able to affect the past does not obviously imply being able to change it. In the grand scheme, though not from Reese's timeline, he and Sarah conceived John before Reese was sent back, before he himself was even conceived. If the past cannot be changed, then the Terminator's efforts must, of necessity, fail. However, the machines' metaphysics may descry a loophole neglected by these considerations. For more on time travel, see "Some Paradoxes of Time Travel in *The Terminator* and *12 Monkeys*" by William J. Devlin, in this volume [*The Philosophy of Science Fiction Film*].

eighteen-wheeler, it calls up a gearshift diagram that instantly enables it to drive a double clutch. Scary stuff, this: this alien, capable, ruthless consciousness. What makes the Terminator's physical threat so horrific is the notion that what drives the physically superior, lethal machine is, in relevant though not all respects, a superior, more efficient mind, a consciousness with which we simply cannot connect. As Reese says, "It can't be bargained with, it can't be reasoned with, it doesn't feel pity, or remorse, or fear, and it absolutely will not stop, *ever*, until you are dead."

Whereas the Terminator does not feel pity or fear, we do, not only in everyday life but also in our encounters with fiction. Our emotional reactions to artificial intelligence and its fictional depiction in *The Terminator* will serve as focal points in this essay for examining what is often called the paradox of fiction. In a nutshell, why do we respond emotionally to fictions, things that we know do not exist? Why does the Terminator frighten us? After explaining the paradox in some detail in the next section, I will argue for a contextual solution, one motivated by a divide-and-conquer strategy.[4] What makes *The Terminator* a particular useful paradigm case is that, among various quality science fiction films, it stands perhaps unsurpassed in generating a particularly significant range of certain emotions (fear, pity, admiration, desire). When this range is examined vis-à-vis *The Terminator*, a key assumption underlying the paradox (specifically that emotions are homogeneous in paradox-relevant respects), is exposed as problematic.

Here is a thumbnail sketch of what follows. Sometimes, owing to context or the kind of emotion in question, our response to fiction is not genuinely but rather ersatz or quasi emotional. When the emotional response is genuine, however, we need not believe that the fictional object eliciting it somehow really exists. We might well experience real fear when the Terminator is on screen, even if the pity-like response we have toward its victims is ersatz. Such responses can be rational, furthermore, when the possibilities the fiction presents are in palpable

---

[4]This loosely follows the advice of Jerrold Levinson, *The Pleasures of Aesthetics* (Ithaca, NY: Cornell University Press, 1996), 303. Levinson suggests that different approaches to the paradox should be incorporated into a general solution to it. Importantly, however, a contextualist solution is not a general solution, although it does provide a framework for a variety of particular solutions. Peter Lamarque reads Levinson's position as broadly in line with Kendall Walton's, which will be discussed in the next section and which is decidedly not contextualist. Peter Lamarque "Fiction," in *The Oxford Handbook of Aesthetics*, ed. Jerrold Levinson (New York: Oxford University Press, 2003), 388.

measure plausible. Increased awareness of the possibility of artificial intelligence makes the scenario presented by *The Terminator* seem less like science fiction and more like science future. There is room to speculate, in offering an alternative solution, that since fictional entities can serve to focus abstract, emotionally relevant concerns, they not only furnish us with but also in some sense are, and not to the detriment of our reason, objects for these emotions.

The Paradox, Suspending Disbelief, and Make-Believe

Without reflecting on it too much, we might assume that our emotional responses to fiction, including movies like *The Terminator*, are unproblematic. Getting caught up in a good story often means, among other things, being moved by fictional characters, by what happens to them, by what they do. So the Terminator makes us feel fear, Sarah pity, and Reese admiration. What could be more straightforward? On reflection, however, there is something odd, even paradoxical, about our emotional responses to fiction. The paradox is generated by the following three individually probable, almost axiomatic, but mutually inconsistent propositions:

1. Readers or audiences often experience emotions such as fear, pity, desire, and admiration towards objects they know to be fictional, e.g., fictional characters.
2. A necessary condition for experiencing emotions such as fear, pity, desire, etc., is that those experiencing them believe the objects of the emotions to exist.
3. Readers or audiences who know that the objects are fictional do not believe that these objects exist.[5]

In sum, how is it that we feel emotions toward things we know do not exist, when such feelings apparently depend on believing they actually do exist? How is it, for instance, that we can feel fear toward the Terminator when, as far as we know, there is no such thing? Formally speaking, there are eight ways of handling the problem, not all of them equally plausible. We might try to reject any one of the three propositions (three), any pair of the three (three), all three (one), or none (one), in the last case concluding unpalatably that something

---

[5]Lamarque, "Fiction," 386.

in our engagement with fiction is fundamentally irrational, since the triad implies that an emotional response to fiction involves the belief that a fictional entity, in the same sense, both does and does not exist. I will focus on the first and last maneuvers here, that is, attempts to reject a single proposition and, barring that, acceptance of the verdict that emotional engagement with fiction is irrational.[6] This will help to motivate a contextual solution that limits the scope of propositions 1 and 2 without rejecting either.

A solution with traditional flavor but without much current support is to reject proposition 3, on the grounds that when audiences are truly engaged in a fiction, they come to believe, in a way, or half believe that the fictional characters and goings-on are real. When we fear the Terminator, we come somehow to believe, or half believe, that it is real. This should recall Coleridge's famous "willing suspension of disbelief," although the positions are not the same. Whereas naive audiences might briefly mistake fiction for fact, "sophisticated audiences, to whom the paradox is addressed, do not come to believe, or even to half-believe, that fictional characters are real people, though such characters might *seem* quite real."[7] However real the Terminator seems, no one really believes or half believes it to be real. No wonder that such a solution strikes one as, to say the least, implausible. It is. But we should take pains not to conflate this proposal, rejecting proposition 3, with the notion of suspending disbelief.[8] Since the disbelief in something fictional is the belief that it does not exist, suspending that belief does not imply the belief that it does exist, just as a suspended atheism fails to imply theism. The disbelief simply fails to play the active role in one's mental economy that it will in other contexts. One simply goes offline. To get caught up in *The Terminator*, it might help not to worry about the metaphysical status of the things I seem to see. That would distract from the entertainment. But again, this does not mean that I believe what I see. So Coleridge's view is a rejection not of proposition 3 but of proposition 2, a type of solution to which we will return in later sections.

Audiences typically do not believe that fictional objects are real (except, insofar as the stories exist, as fictions; the Terminator is not real, but *The Terminator* is). It may also be that our emotional re-

---

[6]Colin Radford, "How Can We Be Moved by the Fate of Anna Karenina?" *Proceedings of the Aristotelian Society*, suppl. vol. 49 (1975): 67-80.

[7]Lamarque, "Fiction," 387.

[8]Contrast with ibid., in which the suspended disbelief view is closely associated, if not identified, with the rejection of proposition 3.

sponses to fiction, in some sense, are not real either. In other words, the culprit may be proposition 1. To clarify this, on Kendall Walton's account of artistic representation and engagement as a kind of make-believe, we do not have bona fide emotional responses to fiction, even if those responses feel like the genuine articles.[9] At most we experience quasi fear or quasi pity, ersatz admiration. Whereas real emotions dispose us to take action, fleeing the fearsome, comforting the pitiable, and so on, our affectively charged responses to fiction do not, in any ordinary way, so dispose us. When the Terminator comes on screen, no one flees the theater or switches off his or her DVD or VHS player. Still, knowing that the fiction is a fiction, in concert with bona fide emotional response, would seemingly suffice to explain the dispositional lack. Critics observe that the make-believe account requires both that audiences be systematically mistaken about their emotional states in encounters with fiction, unable to distinguish, say, between real and fake pity, and that, for instance, horrific scenes cannot yield genuine fright, only an undetectable knockoff version.[10] The critics are certainly onto something. The outright rejection of proposition 1 is probably not viable as a general solution to the paradox. By the same token, we should not be too quick to dismiss its potential use in a curtailed and slightly modified form, as we shall see.

Divide and Conquer I: Context and Emotional Kinds

Obviously it is not true that everyone always responds emotionally to fiction in encounters with it. Watching *The Terminator*, a person need not be moved to fear the Terminator, pity Sarah, or admire Reese. For a number of reasons a fiction, even a well-done fiction, may leave us cold or, worse, turn us off. Such cases are not central to the paradox, however, which does not concern the failure to respond emotionally, or such emotional response as we might have to the film qua film—liking it, for example, or disliking it—but rather responses to fictional elements in it, the difference between disliking *The Ter-*

---

[9] Kendall Walton, "Spelunking, Simulation, and Slime: On Being Moved by Fiction," in *Emotion and the Arts*, ed. Mette Hjort and Sue Laver (Oxford: Oxford University Press, 1997), 38.

[10] Lamarque ("Fiction," 387) cites various critical responses to this effect, including his own *Fictional Point of View* (Ithaca, NY: Cornell University Press, 1996).

minator and disliking the Terminator.[11] It is the standard cases that count, those in which we are engaged with and actively appreciate a fiction. However, appreciatively engaging a fiction does not by itself imply emotional response to any, much less all, of its fictional elements. Assuming that we do respond emotionally to "fictionalia" in a broad range of standard cases, this is perfectly compatible with there being a broad, complementary class of standard cases in which we fail to so respond, in which we do imagine or pretend that we are having the relevant emotions. If we grant that audiences often feel real pity for Sarah or fear of the Terminator, it is no less plausible that audiences often, in some sense, merely imagine doing so, approximating the mindset, perhaps as a way of facilitating aesthetic pleasure in the absence of robust emotional engagement. The key difference between this perspective and Walton's, aside from its being offered as only a piece of the completed puzzle, is that audiences clearly know the difference between feeling and faking it, between genuine emotion and make-believe as considered here. More important, we leave the door open for plenty of real emotional responses in a broad range of standard cases.

If it is at all plausible to suppose that our emotional responses to fiction can be bona fide and, by turns, discernibly make-believe, this is likely not only because of the different contexts of engagement but also because of differences in emotional kind, the type of emotion in question being more significant than is usually supposed. As the very formulation of the paradox suggests, proposition 1 especially, there is a tendency in the literature to treat various candidate emotional responses to fiction the same, as if there were no paradox-relevant differences among what seem to be, in the case of watching *The Terminator*, my pity for Sarah, admiration for Reese, fear of the Termina-

---

[11]Perhaps we can avoid the paradox altogether by defending the idea that we never respond emotionally to the fictional elements in a work but only to a work's general capacity to entertain us and specific means of doing so; whereas the fictional elements may engage our imaginations unemotionally, it is the work and the engagement itself which serve as the objects of real emotions. As with the make-believe approach, this amounts to a rejection of proposition 1. But we are not forced, as on the make-believe account, to say that we have quasi emotions that cannot be distinguished from real ones. We simply find other objects for real emotions, the artworks themselves. This move is similar to that of identifying real-world counterparts to fictional characters as objects of fiction-generated emotions. An important difference, however, is that even where there are no plausible real-world counterparts (as in various types of unrealistic fiction), the art-as-emotional-object view can still hold.

tor, and desire for Ginger (Sarah's roommate). Emotions are assumed to be homogeneous in paradox-relevant ways, but this presumption of affective unity is ultimately untenable. Some emotions, like fear and desire, are lower, more basic than others, are experienced by a wide variety of animals, require little if any intellectual involvement or cultural understanding, and are rooted in evolutionarily primitive parts of the brain, specifically the hypothalamus and limbic system. Other emotions, such as admiration and pity, are less basic, higher, as they are experienced by comparatively few species, require more cognitive sophistication and cultural participation, and are elaborated from the reptilian brain into the cerebral cortex. Because of the greater cortical involvement and, for that matter, commitment required by higher, nonbasic emotions, it is more than plausible to suppose that it is in connection with them, and not with the more basic emotions, that make-believe responses to fiction predominate. Maybe we cannot often or ever literally pity Sarah or admire Reese, as pity and admiration more intuitively seem to require an existential commitment, a belief that the objects of the emotions exist, far more than do feelings of fear and desire. It certainly seems to me that I do not literally pity Sarah, although by contrast I do acknowledge a mild, somewhat excited fear when I see the Terminator on screen, scored by an unnerving four-beat-cycle artificial heartbeat. Note that the criticism of the make-believe view, discussed above, that it is unrealistic to say that we never get genuine emotions vis-à-vis known fictions, is most persuasive when considering the lower, basic emotions, and not nearly so otherwise.

If the preceding discussion is on the right track, then in many contexts, and for what I am calling higher emotions typically, we have reason to reject proposition 1 as requiring that audiences often experience genuine pity, admiration, and the like toward objects they know to be fictional. We also have reason, in many other contexts, and for what I am calling lower emotions, to maintain proposition 1 as requiring that audiences often experience genuine fear, desire, and the like, *toward*—the preposition will become all-important later on—objects they know to be fictional. We must seek the solution for lower emotions elsewhere, and this is next.

Divide and Conquer II: No Object Required

So far we have half of a contextual solution to the paradox. While we might sometimes think we feel genuine pity for Sarah or admiration for Reese, we usually and knowingly do not, because of the existential presupposition of higher emotions. This leaves lower emotions, such as fear toward the Terminator, unaddressed, since the persuasiveness of a make-believe-style solution depends on their exclusion. With propositions 1 and 3 intact, to avoid the implication that engagement with fiction is fundamentally irrational, we must look to scotching proposition 2 as it stands, according to which having an emotion implies belief that the object exists. The rejection of 2 normally involves some species of so-called thought theory, according to which the fiction-to-emotion process, mediated by thought, may and often does occur without concomitant existential belief. The thought alone is sufficient. Fear is caused by thoughts about the Terminator, but it is not fear *of* the Terminator, the *of* phrase deflated to specify nothing more than nonrelational content.[12] In other words, my fear *toward* the Terminator, caused by the film and mediated by thought, is mere Terminator-fear, literal fear, but not literal fear of the Terminator. If emotions can be felt without the existential commitment required by proposition 2, then the proposition is false.

We have already seen that this is a more persuasive view of lower emotions than it is of higher emotions. Thought theory probably cannot provide a complete solution on its own, for reasons that complement those evincing the same outcome for the make-believe approach. Where the make-believe approach succeeds, thought theory fails, and vice versa. Thought theory will prove at best a good account only of the lower emotions. Whereas the make-believe approach, dispensing with genuine emotion, need not posit objects of quasi emotion, especially when construed as discernible as such by their subjects, as I have urged, the thought theorist is obliged to explain away the apparent need. Indeed, the standard worry about thought theory is that

---

[12]Variations on the theme are elaborated in Noël Carroll, *The Philosophy of Horror, or Paradoxes of the Heart* (New York: Routledge, 1990); Lamarque, *Points of View*; and Susan L. Feagin, *Reading with Feeling: The Aesthetics of Appreciation* (Ithaca, NY: Cornell University Press, 1996); Edward Gron, "Defending Thought Theory from a Make-Believe Threat," *British Journal of Aesthetics* 36 (1996): 311-12; Eva M. Dadlez, *What's Hecuba to Him? Fictional Events and Actual Emotions* (University Park: Pennsylvania State University Press, 1997); and Robert J. Yanal, *Paradoxes of Emotion and Fiction* (University Park: Pennsylvania State University Press, 1999).

fiction-generated emotions have no corresponding objects, that when I feel, say, Terminator-fear, there is nothing of which I am afraid, apart from, in some sense, the imaginary object, which I seemingly do not take to correspond to anything real.[13] Other than simply insisting that the imagined Terminator is sufficient for my fear independent of existential commitment, one might claim that although there is strictly nothing of which I am really afraid, I am nonetheless afraid of it, in the same way that while it is true that the ancient Egyptians worshipped Osiris, there is nothing of which it is true to say the Egyptians worshipped it.[14] But this reply neglects a crucial disanalogy: the Egyptians believed that Osiris existed; I do not believe the Terminator does. I cannot fear the Terminator in a sufficiently analogous way. There might be nothing real in either case, but the crucial thing is what the parties take to be real.

What we need at this point is independent reason to suppose that lower emotions like fear do not require objects, do not depend in other words on the subject's existential commitment. For starters, as Peter Lamarque observes, "that thoughts [alone] can have physiological effects is well recognized in the case of revulsion, embarrassment, or sexual arousal."[15] We might also observe that certain emotional states, like free-floating anxiety, seem not to require, and perhaps by definition cannot have, an object. As well, the notion that emotions are invariably caused by thoughts is too simplistic if not naive. Neurologically speaking, basic emotional response often precedes thought, occurring before existential considerations can enter in—hypothalamic and limbic first, and only then cortical—and somewhat recalcitrant to such afterward, with or without presumed object. Seeing the Terminator on screen may, in the right circumstances, unavoidably elicit a fear response regardless of one's unshaken belief that it is not real. Not only is existential commitment unnecessary in these cases, so too, at first, is thought. Another, more general, example is fear of the future. The future does not yet actually exist, but prospective events and not yet real things can nonetheless be feared. One might fear artifacts like the Terminator being built one day.

To take an example closer to home, suppose I am awakened one night by a noise, and as a result I am agitated, fearful, and I speculate that someone may have broken in, or that some other danger,

[13]Lamarque, "Fiction," 388.
[14]Gron, "Defending Thought Theory," 311-12.
[15]Lamarque, "Fiction," 388.

some imminent harm, might be in the offing. In this state I might be genuinely frightened, but I do not necessarily believe, and I probably do not believe, that there is something of which to be so. What is implied here is not the belief that there *is* something of which to be afraid but instead the belief that there *might be* something of which to be afraid. The *might* makes all the difference. The possibility of there being something fearsome exists, but the possibly fearsome something need not. We must be careful to note here that the fear and the associated belief are distinct states of mind. It is not as though I fear the possibility of an intruder. Rather, I fear that there actually is an intruder. But I need not believe that an actual intruder is there. The most it seems I need to believe is that an actual intruder might be there. To fear the actuality, one need only believe the (presumably nontrivial) possibility. In fact, if I do believe that an intruder is there, I am likely not to fear it. What I am likely to fear instead is what the intruder will do, but has not yet done, to me or my property. So here again, while the fear represents actual states of affairs that are not yet actual, events that may or may not happen, I need not, and in some sense cannot, believe that what is feared is real.

Artificial Intel and Metaphysical Psych

It appears that we now have a neat contextual solution to the paradox of fiction. For higher emotions, such as pity and admiration, we limit the scope of proposition 1 to exclude such emotions. For the most part, we construe paradox-relevant prima facie cases, such as pitying Sarah, to reduce to quasi emotional states, with the twist that audiences can usually tell the quasi from the real. For lower emotions, such as fear, we limit the scope of proposition 2 to exclude such emotions, holding a modified thought theory, taking thought as sufficient sans presumed extant object to yield real emotion. Possibilities will do. By such means we adopt the strengths of both theories and the weaknesses of neither, as we can ill afford to reject proposition 1 or 2 outright, and we avoid having to accept all three as originally formulated, which jointly imply that human engagement with fiction is fundamentally irrational. But the story does not end here, for while my Terminator-fear fails to imply that I believe that the Terminator both exists and does not exist, it might seem irrational for us ever to respond emotionally to fiction. If proposition 1 holds in a significant, though significantly reduced, range of cases, why should this be so?

Part of the answer might be suggested by the discussion of lower emotions in the section above. Such emotions are designed, and for good reason, to precede thought often enough. The mechanisms of emotion are biologically tailored to serve a number of fairly obvious functions in daily life, and though they frequently stir up psychological conflict and other sorts of trouble, they are pretty good at their job. They have a built-in practical rationality, and this is so even if, in certain biologically unusual domains such as fictional engagement, where makers of fiction play on such mechanisms, they systematically fail. So the mechanism is not irrational generally speaking, for failure in select domains can be counted as a byproduct of what makes the mechanisms successful in domains of more immediate biological significance. But are the mechanisms then irrational within the domain of fictional engagement, where they systematically "fail" when fiction moves them, and consequently us, to experience real emotion? Arguably not. Perhaps real emotions reinforce the lessons gleaned from fiction in ways that quasi emotions simply cannot or cannot nearly as well. We might mention, too, Aristotle's familiar notion of catharsis—getting out the bad blood—or speculate, relatedly, that fiction exercises our emotional mechanisms, calibrating them for the real world, getting them set for life.

These considerations, while legitimate, might seem to miss the point. It is not the pragmatic, instrumental value of the mechanisms of emotion or the lower emotions they yield in engagement with fiction that matter but rather whether such emotions in such contexts are really warranted, justified, assuming it is appropriate to speak of the pure, abstract rationality of feelings in this way. Analogously, while the belief in the divine might be pragmatically vindicated—easing one's anxieties, furthering one's interest à la Pascal's wager—this does not mean the belief has any objectively rational justification. Maybe my Terminator-fear precedes thought and is to some extent resistant to thought's influence. Emotions may be cognitively impenetrable to a significant degree. But aside from the aesthetic pleasure facilitated by and incorporating my fear, what justification if any do I have for maintaining the emotion, for not trying to quell it to the extent that I can?

It might seem senseless to talk of the justification of emotion as analogous to the justification of belief. But a fear of Terminator-style tech noir seems, and is, far more appropriate in the context of a worldview that admits the possibility of artificial intelligence than in that of a worldview that does not admit it. A naturalist, who believes that everything in the universe, consciousness included, stems from physical states and processes, is apt to admit, almost by default, the possibility of artificial intelligence, of being able ultimately to build something like the Terminator. A dualist, by contrast, who conceives of the mind as a spiritual entity, one not physically determined, is liable, as of necessity, to deny the possibility. Assuming that both views are justified provisionally, if not when all the chips are down, the question of whether a *Terminator*-induced fear is rational ultimately depends on the subject's belief system, specifically the core of his or her conceptual framework, a question of metaphysical psychology. It is more rational for a naturalist to feel Terminator-fear than it is for a spiritual dualist.

At this point the discussion seems to have skirted a crucial if not directly germane issue: is artificial intelligence possible, really possible? The short answer is yes.[16] But this is not the relevant point here. The point is that experiencing Terminator-fear when watching *The Terminator* does not imply either unwarranted existential commitment or the subject's irrationality. Such emotions may be beyond critical censure anyway, even though there would still appear to be a marked difference between the naturalist's fear and the dualist's. The first would be more appropriate, more fitting, than the second. The upshot of this is that in entertaining genuine and genuinely fearsome possibilities relative to a subject's metaphysical psychology, there is nothing amiss in, and much to be gained by, the subject's responding accordingly.

Speculative Outro

Although I have offered a contextualist solution to the paradox of fiction, the search for a uniform solution is both psychologically tempting and perhaps theoretically desirable. One possibility that has not yet been raised is that we consider real-life counterparts to stand in as the objects of fictionally generated real emotions.[17] The standard exam-

---

[16]For those interested in whether artificial intelligence is possible and, if so, what that might mean for the philosophy of mind, a place to start is Jason Holt, *Blindsight and the Nature of Consciousness* (Peterborough, ON: Broadview Press, 2003), 100-101, 143 n. 4.

[17]Barrie Paskins, "On Being Moved by Anna Karenina and *Anna Karenina*,"

ple in much of the literature on the paradox is the pity we (allegedly) feel for Tolstoy's tragic heroine Anna Karenina. On the standard counterparts interpretation, the pity we feel is real, but it is not really for Anna Karenina but rather for actual, real women who suffer similar misfortunes. This tack might seem less plausible in the case of science fiction, for the predicaments found in science fiction are unlike those in which any real person has been. Many people have become suicidal after being jilted by their lovers; no one has ever been hunted by an artificially conscious Terminator. Anna Karenina's shoes are often filled; Sarah Connor's, never. However, at the right level of abstraction, Sarah's predicament is quite familiar. She is overwhelmed by unrelenting imminent mortal threat, and many real people have been there. From another angle, although Sarah's specific predicament has no real-world counterparts as yet, it has an inordinate number of possible-world counterparts, and as argued above for the lower emotions, possibilities suffice. Perhaps they suffice for higher emotions too. Even if possible worlds exist in some sense, however, they do not exist in the actual way this world does. But no matter how we "modalize" the counterparts, this maneuver fails to account for the apparent particularity of our response to fictional characters: "We pity Anna Karenina herself, not just *women in Anna Karenina's predicament*."[18] The problem, in other words, is that whatever might plausibly serve as the objects of real emotions generated by encounters with fiction are going to be too diffuse, too general, for the specificity of such responses. Such specificity might attach only to higher emotions, however, whereas the lower emotions are and ought to be more diffused. My Terminator-fear is clearly not of the particular Cyberdyne Systems Model 101 that targets Sarah but rather of tech noir generally. If this is so, then we simply return to the paradox and the contextual solution.

This return might be hasty, however, so let us speculate a little. Perhaps insights from the counterparts perspective, in abstracted or modalized form, can be blended with the concern motivating the specificity objection. Even in standard thought theory, there is a specific object, albeit unreal, toward which fiction-born and fiction-borne emotions alike reach. Our Terminator-fear is not strictly of, but is directed

Philosophy 52 (1977): 344-47; and William Charlton, "Feeling for the Fictitious," *British Journal of Aesthetics* 24 (1984): 206-16.

[18]Lamarque, "Fiction," 388 (italics in original). Lamarque cites Bijoy Boruah, *Fiction and Emotion: A Study in Aesthetics and the Philosophy of Mind* (Oxford: Clarendon Press, 1988).

toward, the fictional object, thoughts of which inspire the fear. The Terminator, as depicted, gives us specificity, the counterparts plausibility. The key is to get the two together. One approach would be to liken the fictional object to a lens through which we metaphorically see the counterparts, just as views through microscopes depend as much on the lens power as on the nature of what is seen. Fear is directed toward the Terminator but does not stop there. In either case what is "seen," if not literally seen, can be presented and viewed in other ways, by other means, but in both types of engagement, we achieve a kind of situational union of the instrument of viewing and the thing or things viewed, even if the lens is less object than, in the right sense, objective. A somewhat different though related approach would be tantamount to identifying fictional objects with their counterparts. This might seem completely absurd, unless one considers that we can deploy a notion that unites the generality of a type (subsuming the counterparts) with the particularity of a token (a specific fictional object). I speak here of archetypes, which are particulars with universal punch, tokens that do not merely instantiate or even represent but rather embody their corresponding types. The Terminator, then, as fictional, may nonetheless be said to embody, as an archetype, and so in a sense *be*, the object of our fear; likewise for our pity of Sarah and our admiration of Reese. Although we do not thereby think that the Terminator actually exists as such, that is, without archetypal endowment, except as a fiction, in this sense the Terminator *is* tech noir, the object of our fear. Apart from presentation and representation, the fiction is the possibility.

What I have offered here, then, are two alternative solutions to the paradox of fiction, one straightforwardly contextual, the other, though highly speculative, more unified, an account that otherwise might be marshaled to defend thought theory, or the contextual view, from objections levied against the first but applying, it seems, to both. The speculative solution, I expect, will win few converts, as it is provocative but clearly needs much more fleshing out. I offer it to spur further creative thought on the paradox, not as a final solution. Perhaps, like many movies, books, and theories, it will itself prove, in this respect, at least a useful fiction.[19]

---

[19]Thanks to Steven M. Sanders for helpful comments on an earlier draft.

10 THE HITCHCOCK CAMEO: AESTHETIC CONSIDERATIONS

> Hitchcock's cameos are self-publicizing
> jokes and ironic punctuation marks, no
> question about it. They also have perkily
> nondramatic and illusion-breaking qualities.
> Yet our willingness to point and chuckle at
> them needn't stop us from seeing them as
> something more resonant.
>
> —David Sterritt, *The Films of Alfred Hitchcock*

Good evening.

I'd like to discuss a subject of great personal interest, and not without a certain philosophical purchase: Alfred Hitchcock's cameo appearances in his films.[1] The danger of discussing this subject, especially from an aesthetic point of view, is that one may say something both amusing and instructive. However, I'm willing to take the risk.

The Hitchcock cameo is among the best-known, yet one of the least appreciated, elements of his work. Even those who've never seen a single Hitchcock film have some inkling that, *were* they to watch one, they'd be liable to see his unmistakable figure pop up at some point. Those who've seen several of his films can recall a cameo or two, and true fans have their favorites: appearing in a newspaper ad in *Lifeboat* (1944), carrying a double-bass in *Strangers on a Train* (1951),

---

[1] For an extensive list of Hitchcock's cameos, see Robert A. Harris and Michael S. Lasky, *The Complete Films of Alfred Hitchcock* (New York: Citadel Press, 2002), p. 248. For a more comprehensive list, go to http://hitchcock.ru/cameos/. For better quality visuals, try http://hitchcock.tv/cam/cameos.html.

appearing in a reunion photo in *Dial 'M' for Murder* (1954), sitting next to Carry Grant on a bus in *To Catch a Thief* (1955), leaving a hotel room and looking at the camera in *Marnie* (1964), getting up out of a wheelchair to shake someone's hand in *Topaz* (1969). But while a great many know about the cameos, few appreciate them as anything more than a gimmick, part of Hitchcock's signature, yes, ironic and sometimes amusing, but often to the detriment of the films' tension and drama, a superfluous, rather idiosyncratic element with little redeeming value.

Given this impression, the cameos present something of a mystery. What are they *doing* there? What's their significance? What was Hitchcock trying to do? Did he succeed? How could the "Master of Suspense"—of all people—include an element in his work, not once, but time and time again, that detracts, even briefly, from suspense, the very thing of which he's the undisputed master? Is there some other function they serve that somehow redeems them?

Enter a Silhouette in Profile (Stage Left)

The TV show *Alfred Hitchcock Presents* (1955-1961) always began with an introduction by Hitchcock, often a sort of faux lecture. I'll begin with a lecture too, though not a faux one. It will be both dry as Hitchcock's and, if less amusing, reasonably brief. Since we'll be applying an examination of the cameos to theories of how to interpret art, we should start by getting a sense of what such theories are.

Certain aspects of art are *beyond* and come *before* interpretation, *beyond* in that they're matters of evident fact not open to dispute, and *before* in that they're what the interpretations are interpretations *of*: the lines and colors in a painting, the words that make up a poem, the frames and scenes in a film—the data of art. Interpretations are hypotheses about what these data mean, and theories of interpretation tell us how to formulate and justify these hypotheses.

There are three basic theories about how art should be interpreted. According to Intentionalism, an artwork means what the artist intended, and so interpretations should be guided by what we can discover about the artist's intent.[2] Interpretations that don't mesh with

---

[2] See Steven Knapp and Walter Benn Michaels, "Against Theory," in W.T.J. Mitchell, ed., *Against Theory: Literary Studies in the New Pragmatism* (Chicago: University of Chicago Press, 1982).

the artist's intentions (given by biography or psychology) are dismissed on that basis. According to New Criticism, it isn't the artist but the work itself that fixes its meaning.[3] One way to understand this is by drawing an analogy with the world. Just as the world lends itself to best explanations of the sort achieved in the sciences, so too do the imaginary worlds of art yield best interpretations. Interpretations that don't gel with such quasi-scientific method are discounted on that basis. According to Subjectivism, an artwork's meaning isn't artist- or work-based but audience-based, a function of how the work is received.[4]

Each of these interpretive frameworks has plusses and problems. Intentionalism has appeal because the artist's intentions *cause* the work to be, and to be what it is, in the first place, and if we know what the artist had in mind, if we know the vision, interpreting the work becomes pretty straightforward. On the other hand, it seems we can, and often do, interpret an artwork in ignorance or even violation of the artist's intentions. That's part of the appeal of New Criticism, which maintains an artist-independent, quasi-scientific basis for objective meaning in art. But here's where Subjectivism gets its foothold. Art seems open to a variety of different interpretations, and many interpretive disputes in art seem unresolvable. Maybe there's no fact of the matter about the meaning of art. Let the audience make of it what they will. The problem here is that it seems that *anything goes*, and while art may be open to different interpretations, nothing's *that* open.[5] Something would be clearly amiss if I interpreted Hitchcock's *Psycho* (1960) to mean "Jason Holt rules!"

These options are often taken to be mutually exclusive. The meaning of art is held to be given by *either* the artist's intentions, the work itself, or audience response. One and only one of these can truly ground meaning in art, because whichever is the right one, the other two will, often enough, conflict with it (or so it seems). Using the Hitchcock cameo as a case study, we'll see that this point of view is probably too simple.

[3]See the classic W.K. Wimsatt and Monroe C. Beardsley, "The Intentional Fallacy," in *The Verbal Icon: Studies in the Meaning of Poetry* (Lexington: University of Kentucky Press, 1954), pp. 3-18.

[4]See Roland Barthes, "The Death of the Author," in his *Image-Music-Text* (New York: Hill and Wang, 1977).

[5]I've barely scratched the surface here. For more detail, try my "The Marginal Life of the Author," in William Irwin, ed., *The Death and Resurrection of the Author?* (Westport: Greenwood, 2002), pp. 65-78.

The Joke

We'll start with the most obvious interpretation of the cameos—they're jokes. When we see Hitchcock appear in his films, we're often inclined to chuckle, especially when the Master's obviously poking fun at someone, often himself. When we see him in *Lifeboat*, in a newspaper ad for "Reduco," a fictional weight-loss product, or in *Strangers on a Train*, carrying a double-bass, he's the butt of his own body type jokes. He makes fun of his other human frailties in *Blackmail* (1929), being bothered by a child, in *Stage Fright* (1950), staring at Jane Wyman, in *North by Northwest* (1950), missing a bus. Cameos like these can easily be interpreted as Hitchcock trying to establish a rapport with his audience. His more ordinary cameos, walking by or standing in the street, are similarly inflected if not outright jokes.

But the jokes aren't always on Hitchcock himself. His frequent self-insertions, especially the more mundane ones, suggest an almost anyone-can-do-this lampoon of acting. (Hitchcock is reported to have used the word 'cattle' to refer to actors.) Such commentary at times includes remarks on the films themselves. The wheelchair cameo in *Topaz* is plausibly an expression of Hitchcock's dissatisfaction with the slow pacing of the film. In *The Birds* (1963), he walks out of a pet store with two dogs on a leash, the ordinary counterpoint to what's supposed to scare us in the film, the terror of nature *unleashed*. Such thematic and plot tie-ins can also be seen in the *Strangers on a Train* and *Notorious* (1946) cameos.

His cameo behind frosted glass in *Family Plot* (1976) is undoubtedly an allusion to the shadowy profile opening of *Alfred Hitchcock Presents*. As jokes, or commentaries, or allusions *by* Hitchcock, Hitchcock's intent is required. The cameo in *Strangers on a Train* can only be Hitchcock's joke at his own expense if he meant it that way. (It can be at his expense otherwise, but it can't be *his* joke.) To the extent that the cameos can be so characterized, they lend some support to Intentionalism.

The cameos can't, however, be characterized generally as jokes, commentaries, allusions, and such. Of the over thirty-five cameos Hitchcock did, less than a dozen are obvious jokes, and far fewer among the jokes are clear cases of commentary or allusion. Most of the cameos, even if humorously inflected, don't come off that way. They were intended by Hitchcock to be there, but would we be wrong to draw the parallel between Hitchcock's body type and the double-bass if Hitch hadn't intended it? Does the Master hold us hostage? I don't think so. This will become especially clear once we know how the cameos came to be.

Origins and Development

When I first got into Hitchcock I had the impression, as many do, that he did a cameo in every single one of his films. Then I saw one (I forget which) in which I couldn't spot it, and I found the experience maddening. It was only later that I discovered that though he did a cameo in *most* of his films, he did not do one in all. There were many exceptions. Most of Hitchcock's early films are cameo-free. His first (first two, actually) came in *The Lodger* (1926), followed by more, then less, sporadic appearances, until the 1940s, when they became a constant feature of his films. Why?

It's an interesting story.[6] The early cameos were an expediency. One day, they didn't have enough extras on set, and rather than delay production, Hitchcock stood in. As audiences began to recognize him in his pictures, they grew to anticipate his cameo appearance in subsequent films. Hitchcock obliged, and the custom was cemented as a signature move, one that he retained throughout the rest of his career.

The important thing for our purposes is the order of things. The key step in the cameo's progression from expediency to signature move wasn't Hitchcock's intent. He simply didn't envision the function that the cameos would serve, the significance that audiences would attach to them. Once he knew, of course, he took the ball and ran. But the function and significance were there before he knew it. There was something special about the cameos that the audience gathered first.

Of course it's entirely possible that Hitchcock had some foresight into the role the cameos would eventually play. The "expediency" story might just be window dressing, in which case some revisionist film history would be in order. Were that true, though, we'd expect the early cameos to be far less sporadic. The real question, however, isn't whether Hitchcock *in fact* intended the cameos to play the role they do, but whether we can know what role they play without knowing for sure (beforehand or after the fact) what exactly he intended. And so it seems we can. We can view the cameos as a whole (including the early ones, retrospectively) as having a meaningfulness that outstrips, or at least does not depend on, the Master's intent.

---

[6]Recounted in *The Complete Films of Alfred Hitchcock*, p. 248.

This spells trouble for Intentionalism, and one begins to see where the work itself and audience response come into play. As upfront as Hitchcock was about manipulating the audience, he also deferred— he had to—to what makes them tick, whether or not he managed to envision that ticking. Paradoxically, then, out of Hitchcock's respect for the audience he manipulates so well, he's no less our hostage than we are his.

Where's Alfred?

You remember the "Where's Waldo?" kids' books? Spotting Hitch-cock in his films is a tougher, adult-level version of the same game. You're watching, say, *Notorious*, and you're caught up in the pivotal party scene, and there he is, screen left, drinking a glass of champagne (and foreshadowing a key turn in the plot). The pleasure one feels at spotting him is akin to that of solving a puzzle, or problem. Where Hitchcock will appear in any given film is a sort of mini-mystery, and one feels, almost, an easy-gotten kinship with Hitchcock's unluckier but more tenacious heroines and heroes in solving it, in getting to the *Eureka!*

But this game is a real mixed bag. On the one hand, looking for it adds, beyond whatever empathy we may feel with the characters, a layer of personal involvement, an extra shot of tension. A link between "Will the hero prevail?" and "Will I succeed?" is set. But the game can go too far, even if one doesn't want it to. One may be tempted or forced to devote too much attention to seeking out the cameo, and not enough to what's happening in the film. Not only does spotting Hitchcock dispel some of the tension that the Master has skillfully built up, looking for it can interfere with the buildup itself. To diminish such distraction, Hitchcock started to put the cameos earlier and earlier in his films. Some are still hard to spot (as in *Rope* [1948], where he walks down the sidewalk, at some distance, during the opening sequence, and possibly later where his silhouette may appear, also at some distance, in an apartment across the street), and even in later movies some of them come well into the picture (as in *Family Plot*, his last film, forty-one minutes in).

When one knows there's a cameo, but fails to spot it, one rightly gets the sense that the richness of the film exceeds what one's taken in, one's contingent appreciation, that the film is more than one's made of it. From a New Criticism perspective, playing the game too much, or perhaps even at all, amounts to missing the point. Even from a Subjectivist viewpoint, the game is somewhat but not entirely legit, since Hitchcock is more rewarding (for the subject) when the cameos, inessential to, and distracting from, the narrative as they are, are given marginal attention. From this perspective, both New Criticism, and to a lesser extent Subjectivism, gain some ground.

The Real Deal

As I mentioned earlier, many people think that the cameos either detract from the films, or are a harmless sort of add-on, part of the artist's signature, but not all that important. Either way, on balance, the cameos don't really do the films any great service. In a way this is true, at least on the surface. However, on balance the films are better for the cameos than they would be without them.

We've already gotten the sense that Subjectivism has its limits, that you can't do just *anything* in how you deal with (how you interpret) art. A good case in point is David Sterritt's take on the cameos as Hitchcock's deliberate (intentional) self-insertion as the master of his domain, as the God-like "presiding spirit" of his films.[7] As evidence Sterritt cites the *I Confess* (1952) cameo, in which, I confess, Hitchcock's bearing does suggest such God-like self-casting. But this is a hasty generalization. Not only are many more of the cameos self-deprecating rather than self-aggrandizing, most are quite mundane spots in which Hitchcock presents himself in the near-caricaturish guise of an ordinary person, remarkable only for not being so.

Except on that one occasion (if even then), the cameos just don't function as Sterritt's take on them would lead us to expect. More importantly, the evidence strongly suggests Hitchcock didn't intend them that way either. Just look. The interpretation would have been fine if Sterritt's claim had been merely that *he* finds it pleasing to interpret the cameos that way, irrespective of Hitchcock's intent. But he didn't. The intentional claim doesn't hold, and the work itself doesn't support it.

A better interpretation, I think, focuses on the cameos' mundanity. Hitchcock's walking by or standing in the street, reading a news-

---

[7]David Sterritt, *The Films of Alfred Hitchcock* (Cambridge: Cambridge University Press, 1993), pp. 12, 14.

paper, playing cards, gawking with the crowd at a crime scene, and so on, adds to the films an appreciable touch of *realism* (in the ordinary sense of realistic, true-to-life, not the philosopher's sense of the term as mind-independence). We willingly suspend disbelief in the improbable, exciting action and plot, but recognizing the real person of Hitchcock in a fictional world (unlike, say, the actors, whose characters obscure their real selves, or the extras, who blend with the background, or even other directors when they do cameos, lacking such iconic status), makes the fictional world seem more realistic, the suspense more plausible. The more realistic the salient context, the more, however improbable, plausible the events. As a mundane but recognizable figure in the context of the cameo, Hitchcock orchestrates a piquant collision between the real and fictional world.

To what extent is my interpretation legit? *I* find it piquant, and the films more enjoyable overall, when I interpret the cameos this way. So far so good, so long as I don't presume anything about Hitchcock's intentions, or the work itself as others will or should take it. Not treading on anyone's toes, neither Hitchcock's nor those of other viewers, my interpretation is legit precisely because it increases my appreciation. This may be so even if Hitchcock didn't intend it, and even if the work itself (as others take it) won't sustain it. At first blush, from the perspective of New Criticism, it may seem that the cameos are unfortunate, practically dispensable elements of the films, as they add nothing to, and often detract from, the work as a whole. However, the work itself may sustain my interpretation as a suitable competitor. On my interpretation, the plot-wise dispensable cameos nonetheless add to and cohere with the films as a whole. They add that touch of realism without which, arguably, the films would be worse off. Even as a signature, an add-on, there's a case to be made that films are better with the cameos than they would be without. Did Hitchcock intend it? An interesting question. But really, who cares? It works for me, does no damage to Hitch, or anyone else, plus there's reason to think it may work for others as well.

Da-dum, Da-da-da-da Dum-da-dum

So where does all this leave us? Interpreting art, and the cameos as an illustrative case study, is a more complex, more involved process than may at first appear. All three of Intentionalism, New Criticism, and Subjectivism hold *within their respective domains*: (1) the history and psychology of the artist, (2) treating the work-as-world or best explanation, (3) facilitating aesthetic experience. For example, the joke cameos lend themselves to Intentionalist interpretation, and the apparent superfluity of the cameos to a reading by New Criticism's lights, although interpreting them as adding a touch of realism, while piquant to me (and so supporting a limited Subjectivism), offers a competing account from the perspective of New Criticism.

In a sense, everyone wins, though it may seem to many a hollow victory at best. Some advocates of Intentionalism, New Criticism, and Subjectivism would have it that *their* approach, and theirs alone, holds the key to unlocking the special meaning of art. But in art, *the* meaning is a fiction, a false ideal. While artists, works themselves, and audience response constrain interpretation, none of them should be held full hostage to another. There are many meanings, as we've seen, not all legit, as we've also seen, but nonetheless there's plenty of room for plurality. Problems arise when an approach that works in one domain is presumed to exhaust the field of meaning.

But intentions don't guarantee results, nor results a best reading. It's best in art as life to keep presumption under wraps.

And now, a word from our sponsor.[8]

---

[8]Thanks to both John Mezey and Monique Lanoix for useful discussion, and to the Philosophy Club at the University of Louisiana at Lafayette, where some of this material was first presented.

11 HEMINGWAY'S DEATH IN
The Sun Also Rises

Chapter II of *The Sun Also Rises* contains a frankly existential conversation between Jake and Robert Cohn that includes the following exchange:

> "Listen, Jake," he leaned forward on the bar. "Don't you ever get the feeling that all your life is going by and you're not taking advantage of it? Do you realize you've lived nearly half the time you have to live already?"
>
> "Yes, every once in a while."
>
> "Do you know that in about thirty-five years more we'll be dead?"
>
> "What the hell, Robert," I said. "What the hell." (Hemingway 11)

The last time I read the novel, the specificity of thirty-five years struck me, and I flipped to the front of the book to find "Copyright 1926." Doing the sum was only natural: 1926 + 35 = 1961: *the very year Hemingway committed suicide.* I was stunned at this, at what is, if nothing else, a chilling collision of biography and text, a coincidence of such aesthetic power one almost has to doubt it really could be merely that. To be clear, it might only be a coincidence, but it also may not be, and the latter possibility is, to say the least, aesthetically provocative.

There might be quibbles, though, about the math, which call into question whether this even counts as a true coincidence. Cohn says that they will be dead not in, but in *about*, thirty-five years, which blurs things a bit, though it would jar the reader for Cohn to be more precise, and not qualify accordingly. Also, Hemingway's death might have come thirty-five years from the time of publication, but probably not from the time of writing, although he certainly could have allowed for such a time lag in finalizing the manuscript. Another complication is that Jake's age in the mid-thirties fails to coincide with Hemingway's late-twenties at the time, although there seems little point in denying the plausibility that Jake is interpretable as Hemingway's literary stand-in, despite other clear divergences of the character from the author.

The more difficult and interesting question is not whether it is a coincidence but rather how best to interpret the coincidence. I assume for now we lack the biographical data to answer such a question unequivocally in terms of Hemingway's intentions, except perhaps as might be inferred from, among other things, the text itself. Even with such data, we might try to deny the apparent significance in terms of a "text only" view of interpretation that would, as a matter of principle, reduce to mere coincidence something that is clearly otherwise.

In elevating the already high esteem in which we hold the novel, there is some aesthetic justification in speculating further on the relationship between the textual excerpt, Hemingway's production of it, and our response to it. We might speculate, for instance, that the excerpt counts as a well-planned suicide note, bizarrely so, but possibly, that in retrospect the suicide becomes the novel's and novelist's own self-fulfilling prophecy. The most extraordinary thing about this interpretive slant is not so much that the excerpt was written so many years before its fulfillment, but that it was written before Hemingway even became *Hemingway*, that nothing in the interim of thirty-five years dissuaded him from fulfilling the promise. The same goes for interpreting the excerpt as Hemingway, true to his roots as a reporter, giving himself a deadline—a date by which he was, by his own choice, to have finished all the work he was to do.

Each of these interpretations has a sort of aesthetic appeal that romanticizes Hemingway the man with a kind of superhuman literary determination. The danger here, though, is in trying to understand the significance of the work too much in terms of the life that produced it, as if we are over-aestheticizing the man at the cost of undervaluing the work, framing it only as a means to authorial appreciation. However, if we reframe the work as an end, as much served by the life that produced it as vice versa, then another, more aesthetically powerful, interpretation suggests itself, one involving literary determination of another kind. Given the excerpt's suggestion of a death to come in thirty-five years, the suicide might be seen as the ultimate aesthetic gesture of completion of a work whose greatness demands such a gesture. This is not the "death" of the author, with the completed work metaphorically killing its writer, but the literal death that completes the work, the true THE END being, not the printed one, but otherwise enacted. Perhaps, it is not too much to say that Hemingway died *from* literary determination: a final touch of self-fulfilling poignancy that was worthy of, in completing it, the great work itself—a death that lived up to its author's most vital moment.

Even if this interpretation is, as I suggest, the most aesthetically rewarding, is it the best interpretation? To the extent that aesthetic reward can serve as a criterion, yes. But the beauty of the "completion" hypothesis cannot by itself rule out, if historical fact is our chief objective, the coincidence hypothesis. But in defense of the notion that the aesthetic view here is plausibly also correct, three comments bear mention. The novel is often held to be a *roman à clef*, which blurs the fiction/biography distinction so that the Jake/Hemingway relationship is rather closer than mere literary alter-egohood. Also, whatever Hemingway's motivation for suicide, it is plausible that he was aware of the timing of his action *vis-à-vis* the excerpt's suggested timeframe, and so also the potential significance of his own nightfall with respect to *The Sun Also Rises*. Consider as well the ambiguity of Jake's response in the excerpt itself. When Cohn says that they will be dead in thirty-five years, Jake replies, "What the hell, Robert.... What the hell." One is tempted to read this as a knee-jerk rejection of Cohn's impolite conversation, and perhaps also as a kind of existential squeamishness. But, although that makes conversational sense, it fails to fit with what we later learn about Jake's character: he is not particularly bothered by rudeness, nor is he unfamiliar with deep angst or racking despair. "What the hell" might also be read as expressing not a reluctant "Why?" but instead more subtly a willing "Why not?" Such considerations point to the possibility that the completion hypothesis, its aesthetic appeal aside, might just be correct. Although the suicide of the man cannot help its tragic aspect, it may also, as the artist's final act, assume a triumphant one.

Apropos of concluding this note is Alain Robbe-Grillet's prefatory instruction to the reader of his novel, *In the Labyrinth*. The reader "should therefore see in it only the objects, the gestures, the words and the events that are told, without seeking to give them more or less meaning than they would have in his own life, or in his own death" (5). One of the remarkable things about *The Sun Also Rises* is how Hemingway managed, coincidentally or incidentally, to include not only his own life, but also his own death. The skeptic can always reply, after Jake, "Isn't it pretty to think so?"—but we might just consider that the point.

Works Cited

Hemingway, Ernest. *The Sun Also Rises*. New York: Scribner's, 1954 [1926].

Robbe-Grillet, Alain. *In the Labyrinth*. Trans. Christine Brooke-Rose. London: Calder, 2000.

12 A DARKER SHADE: REALISM IN NEO-NOIR

Somewhere in between the soft
lies of cinema and the harsh truths
of reality, there exists an element
of realism in film noir.

—*Carl Richardson**

Classic film noir ran from the early forties to the late fifties, beginning with John Huston's *The Maltese Falcon* (1941) and ending with Orson Welles's *Touch of Evil* (1958). We might widen the scope a bit, citing the little-known *Stranger on the Third Floor* (Boris Ingster, 1940) as the inception of the classic period and *Odds Against Tomorrow* (Robert Wise, 1959) as the terminus, but, even without settling the disputes about which should count as the first film noir and which as the last, the historical limits of the period, spanning at most twenty years, are pretty well defined.

Some purists would have it that film noir is essentially circumscribed by these historical limits, that there can be no noir *in any sense* after the late fifties. This view is unnecessarily extreme. Many

---

*My views in this essay owe much to Raymond Borde and Étienne Chaumeton, "Towards a Definition of *Film Noir*," trans. R. Barton Palmer, in *Perspectives on Film Noir*, ed. R. Barton Palmer (New York: G.K. Hall, 1996); Carl Richardson, *Autopsy: An Element of Realism in Film Noir* (Metuchen, NJ: Scarecrow, 1992); and Foster Hirsch, *Detours and Lost Highways: A Map of Neo-Noir* (New York: Limelight, 1999). I thank Mark Conard and Elana Geller for helpful comments. I also thank Elana Geller for seemingly endless hours of viewing and invaluable discussion of classic and neo-noir.

The epigraph to this essay is taken from Richardson, *Autopsy*, 209.

films made since the end of the classic period exhibit such strong resemblance to classic noir that they clearly deserve to be called *noir* in *some* sense. Nowadays, the term is often used generically, applied as much to contemporary films as (retrospectively) to those of the classic period. But, even if noir constitutes a cycle of films (now closed) or a filmmaking movement (now defunct), this is perfectly compatible with certain films made after the classic period being dubbed *neo-noir* (also known as *contemporary, postclassic,* or *modern film noir*). Irrespective of whether film noir constitutes a genre, such modified use obviously does not flout but rather *respects* the historical limits of the classic period.

The question of how to define *film noir*, or even whether it can be defined, is certainly a vexed one.[1] Nonetheless, it is worthwhile developing a working definition. Noir is often characterized in terms of its bleakly existential tone, cynically pessimistic mood, stylistic elements inherited from German expressionism (low-key lighting, deep focus, subjective camera shots, canted angles, and so on), and stories and narrative patterns adapted from American hard-boiled fiction. These facets of film noir, I would argue, fall roughly under the rubric *stylization*, broadly construed. Tone and mood emerge from style, and the story lines of film noir, for all their contrivances, tend to be highly stylized.

Some other important features of noir are less frequently mentioned and tend to be underemphasized, underappreciated, or outright ignored. It is surprising, for instance, that many accounts of noir either fail to mention or pass quickly over the fact that it is essentially (among other things) a type of *crime* film.[2] After all, it was precisely the desire to label and describe what they saw as a new type of crime film that prompted French critics to introduce the term *film noir* in the first place.[3] Another insight from French critics that is often marginalized is the idea that the characters in films noirs are, from

---

[1]See, e.g., Mark Conard, "Nietzsche and the Meaning and Definition of Noir" (in this volume [*The Philosophy of Film Noir*]).

[2]This is disputed by Paul Schrader, "Notes on *Film Noir*," in Palmer, *Perspectives on Film Noir*, 100; and R. Barton Palmer, *Hollywood's Dark Cinema: The American Film Noir* (New York: Twayne, 1994). Schrader gives no examples. Palmer does (e.g., the woman's picture), although these seem to be either crime films or beyond the bounds of film noir proper. If Schrader and Palmer are right, however, the weakened formulation would be that film noir consists *predominantly* of crime films.

[3]See Nino Frank, "The Crime Adventure Story: A New Kind of Detective Film," trans. R. Barton Palmer, in Palmer, *Perspectives on Film Noir*, 21-24.

a commonsense point of view, morally ambiguous.[4] This is almost a platitude, since what most clearly distinguishes noir from, say, the more conventional thriller or gangster film is the lack of clarity with which moral distinctions are drawn. While some noir characters are unquestionably evil, many have their evil somehow attenuated (e.g., by a sympathetic motive or by being fully revealed as such only at the end). More important, without a hero or heroine of ambiguous moral standing, noir simply evaporates.

While it has been recognized as somehow involved, *realism* is undoubtedly one of the more consistently underappreciated elements of noir. Realism in noir extends far beyond the verisimilitude of studio production and location shooting. Not only the settings but also the scenes, the action, the depiction of violent crime, and the characters involved are all quite realistic by and large. (*Realism* here is meant in the ordinary sense of being true to life, facing things as they are, and should not be confused with various more technical philosophical senses of the term.)[5] What prevents a spaghetti western like *The Good, the Bad, and the Ugly* (Sergio Leone, 1966) from being neo-noir, despite its undeniable noirishness in other respects, is that the prowess of the main characters (in particular Clint Eastwood's "Man with No Name") is elaborated well beyond plausibility, mythologized, in fact. Like the spaghetti western, however, one of the most distinctively realistic features of noir is the role (or lack thereof) that values play in the characters' lives. In providing a spectrum of characters that shade from the morally ambiguous through the completely amoral, noir behavior—in terms of motive, action, and outcome—mirrors an often unacknowledged and significantly unpleasant chunk of human existence. The downbeat endings typical of noir are generally far more lifelike than those usually found in alternative fare.

The reason that realism has been underrated, I think, is that it enters into a sort of dynamic tension with the more obvious element of nightmarish, surreal stylization, much of which, however, can be subsumed under realism, especially the sort of realism I focus on here. As Carl Richardson puts it: "The real world *is* shadowy, crime-ridden,

---

[4]Borde and Chaumeton, "Towards a Definition of *Film Noir*," in Palmer, *Perspectives on Film Noir*, 60-62.

[5]More technically, being a realist can mean holding that facts are mind-independent and (relatedly) that truth does not depend on what we can know. It can also mean, more specifically, being committed to the existence of certain kinds of entities (e.g., subatomic particles) or properties (e.g., being morally good).

web-like, amoral, illogical."[6] The tone and mood of film noir are apropos of how things really are, a sense of reality, not distorted, but *conveyed* by expressionist techniques and convoluted plotlines. These capture a psychological realism, if nothing else, a sense of the world as it can be and often seems. The moral ambiguity of characters is no less realistic. But, while the scope and importance of realism in film noir are greater than is usually thought, it is unlikely that all its stylistic elements can be brought comfortably under the heading *realism*. To hedge my bets, my working definition of *noir* will be "stylized crime realism," where each term in the formula is understood as explained above.[7]

In this essay, I explore realism in neo-noir by examining a cross section of films, paying particular attention to the moral ambiguity of characters and the outcome of their actions in the neo-noir world. Not only will this help distinguish noir from neo-noir in a nontrivial way, but it will also reveal a philosophically germane and crucial part of what, all along, has been the essence of noir. While most of the films selected hold a certain charm for me, almost all are uncontested members of the neo-noir class. Collectively, they serve as a representative sample. Where there is some doubt, I speak to it. If there is any glaring omission here, it is the work of Martin Scorsese.[8] However, just as some noir commentators are loath to discuss Alfred Hitchcock, seeing him as sui generis, so too do I demur from engaging Scorsese here.

No More Spades: *Harper* and *Chinatown*

In the early phase of classic noir, the figure of the private detective was most highly visible.[9] So too with neo-noir, which was more or less sporadically produced in the sixties and seventies before being fully revived in the eighties. Leaving aside such interim films as *Shock Corridor* (Samuel Fuller, 1963), neo-noir began with *Harper* (Jack Smight,

---

[6]Richardson, *Autopsy*, 19.

[7]I thank Elana Geller for suggesting this formulation to me.

[8]For a detailed discussion of Scorsese as a neo-noir director, see Richard Martin, *Mean Streets and Raging Bulls: The Legacy of Film Noir in Contemporary American Cinema* (Lanham, MD: Scarecrow, 1997).

[9]For an interesting discussion of the film noir detective, see Jerold J. Abrams, "From Sherlock Holmes to the Hard-Boiled Detective in Film Noir" (in this volume [*The Philosophy of Film Noir*]).

1966). One of the most obvious and, in many ways, best noirs of the seventies was *Chinatown* (Roman Polanski, 1974). Both *Harper* and *Chinatown* are important early neo-noirs. Each is about a mystery-entangled private eye, and each has an ending that is paramount to establishing the significance of the whole.

Harper begins with the private detective Lew Harper (Paul Newman) making a face at the stale coffee he has made from recycled grounds, which leads us to expect a radical departure from the classic noir detective. Even so, and despite the sixties setting, most of the film proceeds like any classic noir. Elaine Sampson (Lauren Bacall) hires Harper to investigate the disappearance of her husband, who turns out to have been kidnapped and is being held for ransom. Sampson's daughter Miranda (Pamela Tiffin) seems to have no interest in the matter, while the houseguest and pilot Allan Taggert (Robert Wagner) seems too eager to help. The real villain, however, is Albert Graves (Arthur Hill), the Sampsons' lawyer and Harper's friend. Graves, having finally killed his employer, is found out by Harper and taken back to the Sampsons' home along with the ransom money.

While Harper encounters the usual cavalcade of noir characters, and although his attitude is more nonchalant than that of the classic noir detective, what sets *Harper* apart, and finally rewards our expectation from the first scene, is the denouement. In a moment of great drama, Harper walks up the Sampsons' driveway, intending to return the money and incriminate Graves, all the while knowing that Graves is aiming a loaded gun at him. Unable to shoot his friend in the back, Graves uncocks the gun, and Harper, hearing this, essentially relents, dropping the money and raising his hands in a half-shrugging gesture of self-mockery, which severely undercuts the drama of the moment, ending the film on an ambiguous, almost absurd note.

In *Chinatown*, which is set in Los Angeles in the late thirties, the private eye Jake Gittes (Jack Nicholson) is hired to investigate the civic engineer Hollis Mulwray (Darrell Zwerling) by a woman (Diane Ladd) posing as his wife, Evelyn. On flimsy evidence, Gittes leaks a story of Mulwray's infidelity to the press, causing the real Evelyn (Faye Dunaway) to confront him. Mulwray turns up drowned in a reservoir, and Evelyn hires Gittes to find the killer. Gittes's investigation leads to Noah Cross (John Huston), Evelyn's father, who is responsible for the ongoing drought in the area and is fraudulently buying up depreciated land. Once romantically involved with Evelyn, Gittes learns that the young woman he saw Mulwray with is Evelyn's sister/daughter and Cross's daughter/granddaughter, Katherine (Belinda Palmer). In attempting to help Evelyn and Katherine flee to Mexico, Gittes fails. Evelyn is shot and killed by police, and Cross, having orchestrated Mulwray's murder, is free to reclaim Katherine, escaping justice entirely.

Harper and Gittes, each in different ways, exhibit the departure of the neo-noir detective from such classic noir counterparts as Sam Spade and Philip Marlowe. While both neo-noir detectives are nominally competent in narrowly defined domains, Harper lacks the sort of integrity that allowed Sam Spade to triumph (although Spade would, no doubt, be more intrigued by Miranda), and Gittes lacks the wherewithal to negotiate the increasingly dark vicissitudes of the neo-noir world. While less capable, less admirable than their classic-era prototypes, they are, for that very reason, more realistic. Efforts to correct injustice often enough fail, and, in the face of this unpleasant fact, sometimes the best that one can hope for is stoic resignation. As Gittes is finally told, there is nothing he can do: "Forget it, Jake. It's Chinatown."

La Nouvelle Femme Fatale: Body Heat and The Last Seduction

While neo-noir began in the sixties, noir's full resurgence had to wait another fifteen years. Noir came back with a vengeance in the eighties with the release of *Body Heat* (Lawrence Kasdan, 1981), at once an homage to and a reclamation of the classic noir aesthetic. One of the mainstays and most salient icons of classic noir was the femme fatale, fatal not only to the sap who falls for her, and whom she manipulates, but also to herself. Neo-noir revamps the femme fatale. She is no less an object of obsession and desire, no less dangerous, than she was in the classic period, only this time around she gets away with it. Where the classic femme fatale suffers for her crimes, her revamped counterpart prospers.

"You aren't too smart, are you? I like that in a man." So says Matty Walker (Kathleen Turner) to Ned Racine (William Hurt) when they first meet up in *Body Heat*. Ned, an affable but somewhat incompetent lawyer, is utterly beguiled, and, after they become involved, Matty has little trouble convincing him that her loveless marriage to rich husband Edmund (Richard Crenna) would be best resolved by murder. As agreed, Ned breaks into their house at night and bludgeons Edmund to death, disposing of the body in one of Edmund's abandoned buildings, which he rigs to burn down. Edmund's new will, secretly forged by Matty on Ned's stationery, is found invalid, and, instead of receiving only part of the estate, Matty gets it all. When Matty fakes her own death and absconds with the money to a tropical island, Ned alone takes the fall.

There is a particularly striking scene when the plan to kill Edmund is set and, in reference to an earlier conversation, Matty gives Ned a fedora reminiscent of those worn by classic noir heroes, many of whom are not only virile, as Ned is, but capable, as he is not. One beautiful shot in the scene has Matty framed by an open car window, and, as the window goes up, she is visually replaced by the reflected image of Ned, wearing the hat, smiling a bit awkwardly but more genuinely than at any other time in the film. Despite the sap's greed and lust for the femme fatale, she seduces him less into crime than into the inflated self-deception of seeing himself as more competent, more capable, than he knows he really is.

In *The Last Seduction* (John Dahl, 1994), a fledgling doctor, Clay Gregory (Bill Pullman), in debt to a New York loan shark, makes a major drug deal. His wife, Bridget (Linda Fiorentino), skips town with the money and lays low in the small town Beston under the assumed name Wendy Kroy. Although Harlan (Bill Nunn), a private detective hired by Clay, finds her, she kills him before he can get to the money. Bridget convinces her new lover, Mike Swale (Peter Berg), that she is selling murder on the side and, promising a happy future together, inveigles him into making the next hit on a certain "Cahill," who is really Clay. Inept and confused, Mike leaves it to Bridget to kill Clay and then is goaded into some role-playing where, Bridget having covertly dialled 911, he "confesses" that he is raping her and has killed Clay besides.

Whereas the classic femme fatale never escaped justice, the femme fatale of neo-noir, more realistically, often does. This theme has several interesting variations in other films. In *Basic Instinct* (Paul Verhoeven, 1992), not only does Nick (Michael Douglas) fail to bring Catherine (Sharon Stone) to justice, but the pair actually fall in love, albeit in a psychosexually obsessive, deranged kind of way. In *Bound* (Andy and Larry Wachowski, 1996) too, not only do Violet (Jennifer Tilly) and Corky (Gina Gershon) manage to steal the money from

Caesar (Joe Pantoliano), but they also fall in love.[10] For this reason, although they are fatal to certain others, it might be appropriate to consider Catherine and Violet *would-be* femmes fatales and not the genuine article. Even so, they illustrate interesting variations on the getting-away-with-it theme.

Chance and Will: *To Live and Die in L.A.* and *Manhunter*

The moral ambiguity of film noir is often a matter of blurring moral distinctions between the nominally good hero and the villain, whose evil, even in extreme cases, is somewhat attenuated. A prime example is the neo-noir work of the actor William L. Petersen, specifically *To Live and Die in L.A.* (William Friedkin, 1985) and *Manhunter* (Michael Mann, 1986). While *Manhunter* is often discussed as a neo-noir, *To Live and Die in L.A.* almost never is.[11] This is, I believe, because it tends to be woefully underrated as a film, a likely result of its darker tone, blurrier moral distinctions, and much more downbeat ending, in other words, precisely those features that make it an even better candidate for noir status. If *Manhunter* is a neo-noir, there is no reason to deny that *To Live and Die in L.A.* is one as well.

In *To Live and Die in L.A.*, Secret Service Agent Richard Chance (Petersen) tries to bring down counterfeiter "Rick" Masters (Willem Dafoe). When his partner, Jim Hart (Michael Greene), is killed following a lead, Chance seeks to bring down Masters by any means necessary. Undercover with his new partner, John Vukovich (John Pankow), Chance arranges a phony buy with Masters. To get the front money, triple what the Secret Service will allocate, on a tip from his informant and "girlfriend" Ruth Lanier (Darlanne Fluegel) he bullies Vukovich into helping him kidnap a shady diamond-buyer. The robbery goes bad. The buyer, who is really an FBI agent, is killed, and Chance and Vukovich, pursued by an army of gunmen (later revealed to be FBI as well), only narrowly escape. At the buy, Chance is shot and killed, and Vukovich follows Masters to an old studio, where, after a struggle, the building burning down around them, Masters is shot and killed.

---

[10] In discussing *Bound*, Mark Stephenson, an acquaintance of mine, quipped: "Of *course* the femme fatale is lesbian. She always was."

[11] It does, however, make several lists of neo-noirs, including Richard Martin's (*Mean Streets and Raging Bulls*, 170).

The moral ambiguity of the film is quite clear. Masters is a failed painter whose expressionist canvases belie the cold, exact precision of his counterfeit work. His often brutal actions always remain within the bounds of a savvy professionalism, and, despite the unconventional relationship that he has with his girlfriend (Debra Feuer), he treats her rather well. By contrast, Chance extorts sex from Lanier under threat of having her parole revoked, and, despite the plausible nobility of avenging Hart's death, he is driven well beyond the pale of professional and moral standards. In terms of noirishness, this ambiguity is surpassed only by the film's downbeat ending. Not only is Chance dead, but, by killing Masters, Vukovich is essentially transformed, his seduction into the noir world now complete. He takes Chance's place in the dark scheme of things, metaphorically *becoming* Chance. As he says to Lanier in the last scene: "You work for me now."

At the outset of *Manhunter*, Will Graham (Petersen), a former FBI agent, is asked to return to work and help profile and track down a serial killer, who turns out to be Francis Dollarhyde (Tom Noonan), a.k.a. "The Tooth Fairy." He consults Hannibal Lecter (Brian Cox), another serial killer, whom Graham had caught just before suffering a breakdown and leaving the FBI. Graham comes up with several new leads by working the evidence, but his real insights come form watching home movies of the victimized families, trying to empathize with the killer, and even pretending to be the killer himself. On the brink of another breakdown, Graham at last realizes that the killer has seen the home movies, and Dollarhyde, an employee of the film-processing lab, is quickly identified. Dollarhyde is found at home just as he is about to kill his coworker (Joan Allen), and Graham empties his revolver into Dollarhyde's chest.

Manhunter is replete with aesthetic niceties, leaving aside the extended scenes in which Dollarhyde is depicted, for all his evil, somewhat sympathetically and Graham's steady progression from third to second to first person in describing the killer's actions. A case in point is Mann's exquisite use of background details and architecture in framing and composing shots as well as his slight, almost imperceptible excisions and repetitions during certain emotionally charged or action-packed sequences. Also notable are various color motifs. The clinical whiteness of the cell underscores the tone, if not the content, of the conversation between Graham and Lecter, each framed in shots from complementary angles by the same prison bars. In the last scene, Graham's son (David Seaman), framed by the homonymous sun reflected in the ocean, is wearing a shirt that matches Graham's but pants that nearly match those of his mother (Kim Greist). Although this ending is somewhat upbeat, the family having been reunited, it is also somewhat grim, as Graham's face is scarred with what could be read as the film's noir "message"—that what it takes to catch a serial killer is tantamount to being one and that, in the final analysis, what separates the two is largely a matter of luck.

The realism of these films is suggested, not only by their grim endings, but also by the moral status of Petersen's characters, both features serving as excellent illustrations of how neo-noir elaborates on the moral ambiguity of noir generally. Such moral ambiguity does not just feel realistic; in the end it *is* realistic. People we encounter in our day-to-day lives are often of morally indeterminate status, either because we have no relevant information about them, or because we have conflicting evidence. To disambiguate, we often rely on moral tests, observing how people behave when it really counts (i.e., when the chips are down). But, even then, results can be inconclusive. In real life, we seldom find heroes who are morally unambiguous holus-bolus. Chance fails the moral test, although his motive is plausibly noble. Graham passes, but only by a whisker, for, to thwart Dollarhyde, he must indulge at great risk his own sociopathic tendencies.

Odd Investigations, One More Time: *No Way Out* and *D.O.A.*

Many classic noirs were remade in the eighties.[12] While most fail to measure up, some actually surpass their originals by a less than narrow margin. This is particularly true, I would argue, of *No Way Out* (Roger Donaldson, 1987) and *D.O.A.* (Rocky Morton and Annabel Jankel, 1988), which are less remakes per se and more reinterpretations of the provocative premises of the classic noirs *The Big Clock* (John Farrow, 1948) and *D.O.A.* (Rudolph Maté, 1950), respectively. In the first, the hero investigates a murder in which he, unbeknownst to anyone else, is the prime suspect. In the second, the hero attempts to solve his own murder.

No Way Out begins with Navy Captain Tom Farrell (Kevin Costner), in line for a Pentagon position under Senator David Brice (Gene

---

[12]No less than eleven remakes in the eighties alone, and nineteen in the nineties, are listed in Ronald Schwartz, *Noir, Now and Then: Film Noir Originals and Remakes (1944-1999)* (Westport, CT: Greenwood, 2001).

Hackman), romancing Susan Atwill (Sean Young), Brice's mistress. Knowing that she has been with another man, Brice kills Atwill in an obsessively jealous rage, Farrell seeing him at her house just prior to the murder. Brice's aide Scott Pritchard (Will Patton) removes incriminating evidence from the scene, and the murder is blamed on Atwill's other man. To keep the investigation in-house, the suspect is conveniently identified as the subject of an unsubstantiated rumor, "Yuri," a Soviet spy allegedly working in the Defense Department. Under Brice, Farrell is assigned to lead the murder investigation/Yuri spy hunt, but there is no corroborating evidence of Brice's guilt, and all the evidence points to Farrell himself. Although Farrell hinders the investigation surreptitiously, a witness who saw him with Atwill catches a glimpse of him in a corridor of the Pentagon, leading to a massive room-to-room search. Dodging the witnesses, Farrell finally manages to escape from the Pentagon just as he is identified as the suspect. He is taken to a safe house and interrogated by agents who turn out to be KGB. Not only is it now believed by the Americans that he is Yuri, but it also turns out against all odds that he actually *is* Yuri.

There are a number of nice things about the film that bear mention. First, several details foreshadowing the twist are subtle enough not to be noticed as significant. At the bar at the posh president's reception where Farrell first meets Atwill, he orders Stoli, a Russian vodka. His landlord, who is perhaps a bit too friendly, has a detectable Eastern European accent. Also, and more centrally, there is a delightful play on the relation between justification and truth. The Pentagon has good reason to believe that Farrell is the one who killed Atwill, which is false, but no good reason to believe that he is Yuri, which is true. That evidence is no guarantee of truth is a lesson worth learning.

Another odd investigation is the subject of *D.O.A.* Dexter Cornell (Dennis Quaid), an English professor and erstwhile novelist, declines to read the first novel of Nick Lang (Rob Knepper), his talented but pestering student, until Nick falls to his death past Dex's office window. Dex later learns that his estranged wife, Gail (Jane Kaczmarek), had been having an affair with Nick. After a night of binge drinking with admiring student Sydney Fuller (Meg Ryan), Dex feels ill and goes to the hospital, where a blood test reveals that he has been poisoned and has only a day or two to live. He returns to Gail's house just in time to see her killed by an unknown assailant. Eluding the police, who suspect him, and with Sydney's help, Dex embarks on a desperate quest to solve his own murder. After a number of false leads, he confronts his seeming friend and colleague Hal Petersham (Daniel Stern), who turns out to have poisoned Dex and killed Nick and Gail so as to plagiarize Nick's novel and publish it as his own. In the ensuing struggle, Dex shoots and kills Hal before staggering to the police station and recording his statement, before his time is up, of the whole affair on video.

Morton and Jankel's *D.O.A.* is presented as continuous with and, at the same time, a departure from Maté's original version. Continuity is established by the basic premise, of course, but more so by the opening and closing sequences in black-and-white: at the beginning, when Dex stumbles through the rain and into the police station, and, at the end, when, his statement concluded, he walks out into the night. Despite minor errors in depicting how such institutions are run, having the story take place in and around the hallowed halls of academe is truly inspired. In many ways, although often in subtler forms, the ivory tower can be just as petty, dark, and sinister as any mean streets.

Moral ambiguity is a key part of these remakes' noir-style realism. Behind our initial sympathy for Farrell lies a niggling doubt (why did he become involved with his boss's mistress?), and, when he is finally unmasked as having worked for the KGB, not only is it revealed that they coerced him, but he also walks out on them at the end. Our sympathy for Dex is likewise diluted by various personal and professional failings. No less realistic are the downbeat endings of both films. The KGB spy escapes, and the professor solves his own murder only and inevitably to die soon after somewhere in the night.

David Lynch: *Blue Velvet* and *Lost Highway*

My working definition of *noir*, again, is "stylized crime realism." In this section, I examine two neo-noirs by David Lynch, *Blue Velvet* (1986) and *Lost Highway* (1997), which may seem, the latter especially, to push my definition to the breaking point. Bearing in mind the dynamic tension between stylization and realism, the former would seem to dominate in Lynch's nightmarish world. But, for all their stylization, for all their surreality, what the nightmares are *about* (inadequacy, betrayal, the evil of which human beings are capable) is as realistic as the nuances of psychopathology that Lynch routinely exploits. The world *is* wild at heart and weird on top.

Blue Velvet begins with Jeffrey Beaumont (Kyle MacLachlan) finding a severed human ear, which he brings to detective John Williams (George Dickerson). Williams's daughter Sandy (Laura Dern) informs him that the case concerns the lounge singer Dorothy Valens (Isabella Rossellini). Posing as a fumigator, Jeffrey enters her apartment and steals a set of keys, but, when he returns to do more snooping, Valens surprises him, and he must watch from a closet while Frank Booth (Dennis Hopper) engages her in sadomasochistic sex disturbingly charged with fetishism and Freudian roleplaying. Jeffrey, romantically involved with Valens, learns that Frank, the leader of a local crime gang in cahoots with corrupt cops, has kidnapped Valens's husband and son—the ear was her husband's—so as to extort sex from her. After Frank takes Jeffrey for a "joyride," brutally beating him, the police raid Frank's place. Frank escapes and hunts for Jeffrey at Valens's apartment, but Jeffrey shoots and kills Frank, and Valens, although her husband is dead, is reunited with her son.

Although Jeffrey is for the most part a sympathetic character, his motives remain morally ambiguous. As Sandy puts it, we don't know whether Jeffrey is "a detective or a pervert." His family, always watching classic noir on TV, warns him not to go "down by Lincoln," the bad part of town, but he does. The ending is so saccharine, so artificial, that it subverts itself. Back in the family, and paired now with Sandy, Jeffrey is reensconced in the absurd surface appearances of a Norman Rockwell version of small-town America, leaving the seething, violent noir world beneath untouched.

In *Lost Highway*, the jazz tenor saxophonist Fred Madison (Bill Pullman), unable to satisfy his wife Renee (Patricia Arquette) sexually, receives from an anonymous source increasingly invasive videotapes of their home, the last of which shows Fred, in a fit of madness, having killed Renee. He is imprisoned for the crime. More and more unstable (and looking a lot like David Lynch), Fred metamorphoses into Pete Dayton (Balthazar Getty) and is subsequently released. Pete resumes his job as an auto mechanic, once back at work meeting and becoming involved with Alice Wakefield (Arquette, again), the girlfriend of the crime boss Mr. Eddy (Robert Loggia). Alice convinces Pete to commit a robbery with her, on the promise that they will use the proceeds to run away together. In the desert, ostensibly to meet a fence, Alice abandons Pete, at which point he metamorphoses back into Fred. He finds Renee at a hotel with her lover, Dick Laurent (Loggia, again), whom he kidnaps and murders. The police catch up with Fred outside his house, and Fred takes off, racing down the highway with a long line of police cars in hot pursuit.

There are several surreal, metaphysically peculiar, even supernatural elements of *Lost Highway*, and these may exclude the film from the neo-noir class or make it at most a sort of neo-noir hybrid. First, there is the loop. At the beginning, someone informs Fred via intercom that Dick Laurent is dead. At the end, it is Fred himself who speaks into the intercom and does the informing. Then there is the mystery man in black (Robert Blake), who seems at one point to be in two different places at once: at a cocktail party with Fred and inside Fred's house. The mystery man apparently represents homicidal jealousy, and this, together with the loop, suggests that Fred's house is something of a metaphor for his mind. He informs himself (i.e., becomes aware) that Dick Laurent is dead. The jealousy raging within him (i.e., at home) is so vivid that he imagines seeing it in the flesh, projecting it into a semblance of concrete existence. The element that is most disconcerting, however, is the pair of metamorphoses. But, at one point, Fred relates, tellingly: "I like to remember things my own way... not necessarily the way they happened." This suggests yet another non-literal reading. Pete's story can be seen as the noir-stylized version of Fred's story as Fred *wants* to remember it. Note that, while Fred is sexually inadequate, Pete is capable, virile. When Pete is working as a mechanic, Fred's jazz piece comes on the radio, causing Pete to have a severe headache. This is the real profession intruding on the imagined one. In the same way, despite the fevered pitch of Fred's imagination, his disappointment forces its way into Pete's story (when Alice abandons him), bringing Fred back, once more, to himself.

Such interpretations give *Lost Highway* a less surreal and more realistic flavor, at least beneath the surface. The same can be said of *Blue Velvet*'s artificial happy ending. Add to this the moral ambiguity of Jeffrey and Fred/Pete, and Lynch's noir-style realism becomes discernible as an element of his oeuvre.

On the Q.T.: *Reservoir Dogs* and *Pulp Fiction*

On the strength of *Reservoir Dogs* (1992) and *Pulp Fiction* (1994), Quentin Tarantino is the standout neo-noir director of the nineties. *Reservoir Dogs* is, somewhat ironically, the quintessential neo-noir heist film, notable for spending, in direct contrast to typical heist films, hardly any time at all on the details of the planning or execution of the crime itself. *Pulp Fiction* is a tapestry of interwoven noir stories whose common thread becomes clear only toward the end. Despite the obviously stylized elements, both films exhibit a gritty realism about criminal violence and its underlying causes. This is particularly evident in the quick cuts to and lingering shots on the physical aftermath of actions whose extreme brutality is triggered by accident as much and as often as by will.

For the most part I will let these films speak for themselves. Up first is *Reservoir Dogs*. Joe Cabot (Lawrence Tierney), a crime boss, and his son Nice Guy Eddie (Chris Penn) bring together an ad hoc gang to pull a jewel heist. Each gang member is given a color code name, including the principals Mr. Blonde (Michael Madsen), Mr. White (Harvey Keitel), Mr. Pink (Steve Buscemi), and Mr. Orange (Tim Roth), an undercover cop. The gang steals the loot but must shoot their way out, scrambling to reunite at the designated hideout, a warehouse. During a carjacking, Mr. Orange is shot and seriously wounded by the driver, whom he then shoots dead. He and Mr. White repair to the warehouse, where Mr. Pink, having stashed the loot, airs suspicions that they have been set up. Returning with a hostage policeman (Kirk Baltz), whom he tortures while the other gang members are absent, Mr. Blonde is shot and killed by Mr. Orange. When the gang returns, Cabot accuses Mr. Orange of being the rat. But Mr. White defends him, resulting in a Mexican standoff in which everyone gets it but Mr. Pink, who runs off with the diamonds, then is possibly shot by the police. Dying, Mr. Orange finally confesses to the wounded Mr. White, who then shoots him as the police arrive.

In *Pulp Fiction*, Vincent (John Travolta) and Jules (Samuel L. Jackson) do a job for their boss, Marsellus Wallace (Ving Rhames), narrowly escaping with their lives. On the return drive, Vincent accidentally shoots and kills Marvin (Phil Lamarr), their inside man, which forces them to repair to a suburban home, where the Wolf (Harvey Keitel), a consultant sent by Marsellus, oversees the cleanup and disposal of the evidence. Vincent and Jules then have breakfast at a diner, which Ringo (Tim Roth) and Yolanda (Amanda Plummer) attempt to hold up. Though Jules gets the drop on Ringo, he lets the couple go, having already decided to quit "the life" himself. Vincent and Jules return to Marsellus, who has just paid Butch (Bruce Willis) to take a dive in an upcoming fight. Perhaps that night, Vincent takes Marsellus's wife, Mia (Uma Thurman), to dinner at his boss's behest. Presumably mistaking it for cocaine, Mia overdoses on Vincent's heroin, and he rushes her to his dealer's (Eric Stoltz) house for a lifesaving adrenaline shot. On a future night, Butch wins his fight, having bet heavily on himself against the highly inflated odds. He meets up with his girlfriend, Fabienne (Maria de Medeiros), at a motel. The next morning, Butch returns to his apartment to retrieve his father's gold watch. By chance, he gets the drop on Vincent, who is staking out the apartment, and kills him with his own gun. On the way back, he runs, again by chance, into Marsellus, whom he tries to run over, smashing up his car. Both are injured, and Marsellus chases Butch, shooting at him, into a shop, where both are knocked unconscious. They wake up bound and gagged. Butch frees himself and returns to save Marsellus, and, in recompense, Marsellus lets Butch go on the condition that he never return to Los Angeles.

Despite Tarantino's bravado in presenting both narratives nonsequentially, their endings are far more traditional than cutting-edge, making his style of neo-noir more the exception than the rule. In *Reservoir Dogs*, no one gets away with his misdeeds, except possibly Mr. Pink, whose levelheaded "professionalism" almost justifies it. Those who survive in *Pulp Fiction* do so on the strength of having somehow redeemed themselves, effectively elevating them *into* a state of moral ambiguity. However, while the ending of *Reservoir Dogs* is appropriately downbeat, the last scene in *Pulp Fiction* is of Jules and Vincent strutting out of the diner, their guns stuck in their shorts, to the accompaniment of an ultra-hip instrumental sound track. Because of this lighthearted, upbeat ending, one might be loath to include *Pulp Fiction* in the neo-noir class. Still, while the "sequential" ending is not downbeat, the "narratival" endings are. Plus, the sequential ending could be seen as making one or both of the following, much darker points: (1) redemption doesn't really matter; (2) the fact that nothing matters doesn't really matter either.[13]

The Darker Shade

There are a number of obvious differences between classic noir and neo-noir. First off, the former films are predominantly black-and-

---

[13] For further discussion of *Pulp Fiction*, see Mark T. Conard, "Symbolism, Meaning, and Nihilism in Quentin Tarantino's *Pulp Fiction*" (in this volume [*The Philosophy of Film Noir*]).

white, while the latter are predominantly color productions. Certain devices, such as voice-over narration by the protagonist, have been largely phased out, except on rare occasions, when the point is to evoke the classic era. The sporadic use of black-and-white in neo-noir, whether throughout the film or in select scenes, also serves this purpose. The sex is more explicit, the violence more graphic, more extreme, and the forces at work behind both are of a decidedly darker hue. The Production Code, under which classic films noirs were produced, severely limited what could be depicted, how it could be depicted, and, perhaps most important, how it all came out in the end. Once the Production Code was superseded by the ratings system, under which neo-noirs were and are produced, the darker shade could be painted in broad brushstrokes. What once had to be suggested could now be shown.

It might seem a trivial matter that the ratings system allows much more explicit sex and violence than the Production Code did. And perhaps it is. It might also seem trivial that filmmakers now have much greater freedom in deciding how plots will be resolved and whether they even will be. But this is not so. Not only can a film be much more realistic generally, but it can also *end* much more realistically. As I said, part of what holds film noir together is the realistic appraisal of people's motives, actions, and outcomes. Often enough, people really do have dark, indeterminate motives, committing shadily suspicious, evil, and excessively violent acts. But, while the outcomes of noir in general are realistically downbeat, the Production Code required classic noir to exhibit poetic justice, "morally permissible" endings where the victims are irretrievably lost or definitively reclaimed and the guilty get what's coming to them. Under the auspices of the ratings system, neo-noirs exploit the much more realistic possibility that, often, the guilty fail to get their comeuppance.

The reason that such endings are more realistic is clear enough. While neo-noir by no means has an exclusive right to such endings, it does serve to reinforce a valuable lesson, especially in light of most mainstream and many alternative films, which are replete with poetic justice. In philosophy, it is common to speak of the naturalistic fallacy, the mistake of inferring what ought to be the case (a value) from what merely is the case (a fact), the illicit attempt to derive *ought* from *is*. The inverse, inferring fact from value rather than value from fact, is hardly ever discussed, although it is equally fallacious. I call this the *normativistic fallacy*. That something should be does not mean that it is or that it will be. Of course, it is also fallacious to infer that, because something ought to be the case, it *won't* be—we might call these varieties the *optimist's fallacy* and the *pessimist's fallacy*, respectively—and so, despite being a corrective to the unwarranted optimism implied by the vast majority of films, neo-noir might be seen as equally erroneous. But neo-noir has the advantage. The foundation of mainstream optimism is patently escapist, whereas that of neo-noir is transparently realist. Neo-noir enjoins us to face facts in a way that purely escapist cinema necessarily denies us. Pessimism is irrational only when the world fails to warrant it.

While neo-noir distinguishes itself from classic noir by showing the normativistic fallacy for what it is, writ large, the prodigal departure seems worthy of its lineage, even somehow a vindication of it. In fact, it could be argued that this most important element of realism was at the very heart of film noir all the way along, its final form, its telos, its ultimate purpose. The fact that it was latent in classic noir and only fully realized in neo-noir is of no particular consequence. Classic noir did scene by scene what neo-noir does throughout, only, because of poetic justice, less consistently. People ought not to have bad motives or commit bad acts, but often enough they do. By contrast, the endings of classic noirs, an artifice of the Production Code and compliant creative intentions, almost always ring a little off, false, not only to life, but, much worse, to themselves. A most unfortunate illustration is *The Postman Always Rings Twice* (Tay Garnett, 1946), an otherwise fine noir that ends with Frank (John Garfield) *explaining*, for the audience, the poetic justice that he has received! The better classic noirs downplay poetic justice within allowable limits, making it seem less a matter of moral necessity or accidental rectitude and more a matter of pure chance, with no significance besides. Notice how poetic justice fades, displaced, almost to the point of irrelevance, at the end of *The Maltese Falcon*, a grimly perfect fit, or *Double Indemnity* (Billy Wilder, 1944), a note so delicate, so poignant, that justice is really beside the point. Realism, about values in particular, has always been an essential part of the essence of noir. Values alone have nothing to do with what really happens.

13 *Twin Peaks*, NOIR, AND OPEN INTERPRETATION

Any fan of *Twin Peaks* who encounters Goya's lithograph *The Sleep of Reason Produces Monsters* (1803) cannot help but see an obvious connection to the landmark TV series; whether series creators David Lynch and Mark Frost had this connection in mind is of little importance. The lithograph depicts a sleeping figure slumped over a desk. From behind, almost out of view, the somnolent head, emerging from an indeterminate place that seems not quite real, are the so-called monsters identified, together with their cause, in the title: creatures far more sinister than their appearance would normally suggest, many of them winged things, owls. The owls in *Twin Peaks* play a similar symbolic role, have a comparable significance. These are not, in either case, the wise Minervan creatures of Western European culture or native North American folklore. Instead they augur ill, harbingers of bad times hooting evil tidings. "The owls," to follow the series motif, "are not what they seem." Indeed.

Evoking a dark, existential atmosphere is one of the hallmarks of film noir, and while it would be wrong, for many reasons, to call Goya's etching "lithograph noir," the application of "noir" to *Twin Peaks* seems far less inapt, not least because it comes much closer to respecting the historical dimension of the term. Purists might demur from using the term beyond the borders of cinema, and even, within these bounds, with reference to films falling outside what is generally regarded as the cycle of classic film noir, 1941-1958. But one of the guiding assumptions of this volume [*The Philosophy of TV Noir*] is that it might be fruitful to view certain small-screen works through the dark lens of those classic films that so clearly influenced them. *Twin Peaks* is no exception; it would not have been possible without film noir. The influence is incontrovertibly strong, the show's noirish tendencies as many as they are diverse. Juxtaposing *Twin Peaks* with the conceptual apparatus of film noir will help foster a greater appreciation of the former and, as side benefits, a richer understanding of the latter and of interpreting artworks generally.

The question is less whether *Twin Peaks* is noir—it almost certainly is not—and more a matter of why and how its undeniable noirishness falls short of pure noir. *Twin Peaks* is rarely if ever discussed by film critics or theorists as a series noir, and this is understandable, despite the substantial influence of the film type on the series. True, *Twin Peaks* has been called noir, for example, in the *New York Times*, and this reflects the recent trend of using the term "noir" more and more liberally.[1] This practice is especially annoying when the label is applied carelessly, overlooking noir's hard-boiled metaphysics, its commonsense, darkly realistic, naturalistic worldview. Arguably the key reason why *Twin Peaks* is merely noirish, and not actually noir, is that it deliberately leaves, even forces, the metaphysics and, correspondingly, the interpretation of it, wide open. Openness of interpretation, by which I mean the multiple interpretability of art, is apparently inconsistent with noir, which is somewhat puzzling. The open interpretability of *Twin Peaks* gives it its aesthetic piquancy, without which the series would surely be inferior. Yet noir, which seems by contrast to *close* interpretation, is hardly aesthetically impoverished as a result.

I will first examine various noir elements in *Twin Peaks*. Next, I will address *Twin Peaks* and noir metaphysics respectively, to explain in greater detail why, despite its noir elements, the series is not noir. By implication, then, I will chasten overly liberal uses of the term "noir." Then I will argue that open interpretation à la *Twin Peaks* is aesthetically desirable and that, appearances notwithstanding, the best films noirs also exhibit, though in a more limited form than this show does, multiple interpretability. In championing open interpretability as aesthetically desirable generally, I will identify its source in what I call the "omissive" aesthetic, the art of leaving some things, some important things, out of art, or including them only implicitly.

---

[1] Specifically, in Timothy Egan, "Northwest Noir: The Art of the Seriously Goofy," 14 July 1991, B1, B20; and Jeremy Gerard, "A 'Soap Noir' Inspires a Cult and Questions," 26 April 1990, C22.

Shades of Noir

Twin Peaks comprises thirty episodes. The pilot was released, with additional footage inconsistent with the series proper, as a movie, *Twin Peaks* (David Lynch, 1990). The series was later followed by the film prequel *Twin Peaks: Fire Walk with Me* (David Lynch, 1992). The series consists, ancillary and relatively minor plotlines aside, of two consecutive narratives that focus, in the bizarre, dreamlike logging town of Twin Peaks, on FBI special agent Dale Cooper (Kyle MacLachlan). The telos of the first arc is to solve, and in a sense resolve, the murder of homecoming queen Laura Palmer (Sheryl Lee), who, it turns out, was killed by her abusive father Leland (Ray Wise). The second pits Agent Cooper against his former partner and arch nemesis, Windom Earle (Kenneth Welsh), whose vendetta against Cooper is ultimately undone not by Cooper but by the dark forces he seeks out to fulfill his own dark purposes. The arcs dovetail around BOB (Frank Silva), the malevolent presence/psychological symbol under whose influence Leland abused and murdered his daughter and who issues from the Red Room/Black Lodge/White Lodge to which Earle seeks and ultimately gains access.[2]

On the surface, these two major plotlines are classic noir crime stories (crime being essential to noir), thus providing a first taste of the noir elements in *Twin Peaks*.[3] The Laura Palmer investigation is more or less a textbook example of the noir quest narrative, in which the hero, typically a private investigator or cop, is brought into a mystery already in progress. He must rely on his special skills and own code of values if he is to crack the case and avoid the dangers along the way. Likewise, the Windom Earle plot is a standard former-partner-turns-bitter-enemy-and-the-stakes-could-not-be-higher story. Though some of the more minor plotlines are far from fitting such classic noir patterns, others fit, almost to the point of cliché, the femme fatale pattern, in setup and development if not in resolution. Other plotlines in the series are similarly noir.

---

[2]The name "BOB" is given in capital letters here as most commentators and theorists follow this convention [apparently established in Jennifer Lynch's *The Secret Diary of Laura Palmer* (New York: Simon and Schuster, 1990)]. The identification of the Red Room with the Black Lodge is straightforward. While it is less clear whether the White Lodge is yet another descriptive name for the same thing, there are several clues in the series suggesting that this additional equivalence holds.

[3]Jason Holt, "A Darker Shade: Realism in Neo-Noir," in *The Philosophy of Film Noir*, ed. Mark T. Conard (Lexington: University Press of Kentucky, 2005), 24.

In keeping with the narrative patterns of noir are the classic character types they require, such as the trench-coated investigator in the labyrinthine world of crime. Agent Cooper fits the bill to that extent, and although his tragic end distinguishes him from his classic predecessors, it puts him in company with Jake (Jack Nicholson) from *Chinatown* (Roman Polanski, 1974) and other neo-noir counterparts. Still, Cooper appears to be too lighthearted a character, too oddball—with often quasi-mystical investigative techniques—to qualify as an updated Sam Spade or legitimate heir to Philip Marlowe.[4] Even the noir patter is left to his FBI colleague Albert (Miguel Ferrer). Similarly, the town of Twin Peaks is positively teeming with actual, virtual, would-be, and will-be femmes fatales. Almost every resident woman has the tell-tale trappings, allure, poses, and behaviors, in fashionable fashion, of the true noir bad girl. For most there is at least one requisite sap, one sucker, although, admittedly, the femme fatale mystique seems less intrinsic to the female characters in *Twin Peaks* than a stylized aesthetic veneer. Along with lawmen, femmes fatales, and the saps who love the latter, sundry criminal lowlifes and highlifes complete the ensemble.

Speaking of stylization, many of the stylistic elements of film noir are liberally sprinkled throughout *Twin Peaks*. Cooper's Dictaphone communiqués to the never-seen Diane evoke the classic noir voiceover, a device used partly, then as now, for the benefit of the audience, although the device was mostly phased out during the neo-noir period. The use of low-key and high-contrast lighting is taken directly from the noir handbook, not to mention subjective and canted angle shots during psychologically or dramatically intense scenes, somewhat disoriented and disorienting, both. Among various different stylistic parallels, two deserve special mention. First, a certain style of jazz music recalls the noir mindset, even, and sometimes especially, where the setting itself does not: both when jazz is used to complement a scene, as with the sax soundtrack to Sheriff Truman's (Michael Ontkean) shadowy, slow-motion drinking binge, and more strikingly as a motif, as with Angelo Badalamenti's oft-recurring "Freshly Squeezed." Second, the use of reflected images, mirror images in particular, to problematize the identity of the reflected subject, is straight out of versions of psychological noir stories, even where the reflection is far from realistic, as in the Leland-BOB and series-closing Cooper-BOB

---

[4]Angela Hague, "Infinite Games: The Derationalization of Detection in *Twin Peaks*," in *Full of Secrets: Critical Approaches to* Twin Peaks, ed. David Lavery (Detroit, MI: Wayne State University Press, 1995), 130-43.

sequences.

Another element of noir in *Twin Peaks* which cannot be ignored is the dark, somber mood, in effect the existential atmosphere that conveys a tragic sense of life, of meaninglessness, the inevitability of despair. In early noir films this sensibility reflected an increasingly pervasive undercurrent of anxiety and uncertainty in American culture during and after World War II. In *Twin Peaks* this feeling is grounded in the main narrative threads but also significantly maintained and heightened by establishing and closing shots of various town and forest nightscapes to the accompaniment of downbeat Badalamenti music. These include slow panning shots across windswept conifers and still shots of traffic lights with no one in the streets to follow them, of the Roadhouse, the RR Diner, and the unremitting waterfall of the Great Northern Hotel.

To some extent, the existential mood of *Twin Peaks* might be seen as undercut by the frequent juxtaposition of such atmospheric shots with more quirky, humorous scenes, which sometimes cross the line into absurdity. Two remarks are in order here. First, the presence of humor, especially dark or absurd humor, has never been inconsistent with a general existential outlook. Indeed, the absurd, both tragic and humorous, is taken to be a fundamental phenomenon by many existential thinkers and writers. Take, for instance, Albert Camus' fiction and philosophy, or Samuel Beckett's tragicomedies. Lest one think, then, that the noir ethos mirrors the purely dark and never the lighter gray side of existentialism, consider the banter between Neff (Fred MacMurray) and Keyes (Edward G. Robinson) in *Double Indemnity* (Billy Wilder, 1944), or the wit and even laughter of no less a hard-boiled type than Sam Spade (Humphrey Bogart) in *The Maltese Falcon* (John Huston, 1941). For those who consider the right tone, mood, or atmosphere to be a crucial part of noir, *Twin Peaks* is a plausible candidate.

Why Not Noir?

So far we have identified a number of noir elements woven into the fabric of *Twin Peaks*: the crime storylines, iconic characters, stylistic elements, and broodingly existential atmosphere. Are these elements, taken together, sufficient to peg *Twin Peaks* as noir? It might seem so. We should consider, then, some preliminary objections to the notion that *Twin Peaks* is noir. First, it might be observed that noir has not only a typical subject, crime, but also a typical setting, the city. Noirs are characteristically urban crime stories; it is the vicissitudes of urban, not rural, life that private eyes and femmes fatales must skillfully negotiate. One could view *Twin Peaks* as noir displaced from its proper home, and all the more unnerving, then, apropos of noir. One could also acknowledge that while noir, even classic noir, is typically urban, it is not essentially so. Consider the rural setting of *The Postman Always Rings Twice* (Tay Garnett, 1946), whose Twin Oaks Diner tellingly prefigures both the RR Diner and the very title *Twin Peaks.*

In "A Darker Shade: Realism in Neo-Noir," I argue that one of the essential elements of noir is realism, not in the technical philosophical sense that one is a realist *about* something, taking that kind of thing to be real, but rather in the more common sense of the term, being realistic about the way the world is, seeing things as they are.[5] I also suggest that a significant dimension of such realism is presenting characters that are evil in some cases and morally ambiguous in others.[6] In his "Moral Clarity and Practical Reason in Film Noir" in the same volume, Aeon J. Skoble argues, correctly in my view, that noir heroes such as Sam Spade, rather than being morally ambiguous, are, or at least can be, good people in, and trying to negotiate their way out of, bad situations.[7] From a certain perspective, my view and Skoble's are compatible. Spade certainly *appears* shady throughout most of *The Maltese Falcon*, not only because he flouts conventional morality, but also because it is not until near the end that he fully reveals himself to be the gritty, noble hero that he is. Such appearances are not just compatible with Spade's underlying nobility, they also, as he himself remarks, help him do his job.

Here it seems we run into a snag for the notion that *Twin Peaks* is noir, for some characters come off as obviously morally good, sullied at most by eccentricity. Although this concern would be largely assuaged by Skoble's characterization of noir characters, Agent Cooper, on the surface, does not fit the mold a true noir hero. Further, whereas Cooper declined, Spade probably would have bedded Audrey (Sherilyn Fenn). Still, although Agent Cooper gleams knightlike, without even a trace of tarnish, in many scenes, the complete picture suggests that he

---

[5] Holt, "A Darker Shade," 24-25, 37-39.
[6] Ibid.
[7] Aeon J. Skoble, "Moral Clarity and Practical Reason in Film Noir," in Conard, *Philosophy of Film Noir*, 41-43.

is far from pristine. For one thing, he has a troubled past, in step with other noir heroes, having previously fallen in love with his partner's wife, a federal witness, who died in his custody. He similarly fails in the Black Lodge in attempting to rescue Annie (Heather Graham); his fear, his failure of nerve, makes him susceptible to BOB and, in the end, turns him evil. On the whole, although Cooper's apparent moral ambiguity is less obvious than that of typical noir detectives, it is still there, if not in spades. He passes the noir moral litmus test.

The Reification of BOB

The question of whether noir constitutes a proper genre certainly is a vexing one, and I will not engage it here. But *Twin Peaks* is such a mishmash, crossing over the boundaries of so many genres, categories, and styles, as befits its postmodern status, that suggesting it is noir in any straightforward sense is bound to raise some hackles, and rightly so. This is not to say that the notion of postmodern noir is incoherent. Far from it: Films like *Reservoir Dogs* (Quentin Tarantino, 1992), *The Usual Suspects* (Bryan Singer, 1995), *L.A. Confidential* (Curtis Hanson, 1997), *Bound* (Andy Wachowski and Larry Wachowski, 1996), and Lynch's own *Blue Velvet* (1986) and *Lost Highway* (1997) are excellent candidates for the label.[8] Much as it incorporates noir elements, sensibility, iconography, and style, however, *Twin Peaks* seems less like a postmodern noir and more like a hodgepodge with noir as merely one among a host of other ingredients. Leaving out categories closely related to noir, including crime, thriller, and mystery, in *Twin Peaks* we have also elements of horror, fantasy, drama, soap opera, comedy, romance, and even western. This cross-fertilization of genres is pivotally reflected in the metaphysical status of BOB. The uncertainty of his status not only lies at the very heart of why the series is not noir, but also, more important, is of independent interest vis-à-vis the interpretation of art. To this we now turn.

It would be helpful at this point to reintroduce the notion of noir

---

[8] A recent discussion of themes, styles, and narrative patterns of postmodern film noir can be found in Andrew Spicer, *Film Noir* (Harlow, England: Pearson Education, 2002), chapter 8. Steven M. Sanders identifies postmodernist epistemological and aesthetic theses and describes how they are exemplified in episodes of *Miami Vice* in "Sunshine Noir: Postmodernism and *Miami Vice*," in *The Philosophy of Neo-Noir*, ed. Mark T. Conard (Lexington: University Press of Kentucky, 2007), 183-201.

metaphysics. As noted earlier, realism is arguably essential to noir. In other words, the world of film noir is a realistic one, a naturalistic one. A general sense of noir is sufficient to establish this claim, and an extensive survey of examples would strengthen it. The noir world is our world, noir metaphysics our metaphysics. The same could be said for noir epistemology, although this is not a central claim, considering my focus. In a discussion of methods of detection in *Twin Peaks*, Angela Hague provides a historical perspective on the matter. She notes that hardboiled fiction inherited from the classical detective story, originating with Edgar Allen Poe and Sir Arthur Conan Doyle, a naturalistic worldview, ruling out all "supernatural or preternatural agencies."[9] We may add that the legacy continues, from noir fiction (that of Hammett, Chandler, Cain, and Woolrich, in particular) to noir film, from noir film to noir TV. Of course there were other influences on the development of film noir—German expressionism, Freudian psychology, and French surrealism, to name a few—but these can be viewed as stylistic expressions, logical extensions, and symbolic manifestations of what, at base, is a naturalistic outlook, as we shall see.

It may be controversial to interpret *Twin Peaks* naturalistically, but it is by no means out of the question. From a metaphysical point of view, the decisive issue is the metaphysical status of BOB and, similarly, where he comes from, the Red Room/Black Lodge/White Lodge. BOB can be interpreted symbolically, and there are many cues in the series and aesthetic inducements for doing so. BOB can be reduced, or deflated, to no more than Leland's and later Cooper's dark side, a representation of the psychopathology that in Leland's case leads to long-term abuse that culminates in the rape and murder of his own daughter. Similar observations can be made about the Red Room, which might plausibly be interpreted symbolically. Granted, symbolism on this scale and of this type is rather uncommon in noir, except in cases of dream and hallucination imagery. But the strangeness in *Twin Peaks* may in fact come to that. Witness the references in virtually every episode to life in Twin Peaks being, or being like, a dream. That aside, there is nothing wrong with distinguishing seemingly non-noir surface data from an underlying naturalistic realm, in which case *Twin Peaks* might be labeled "deep noir" or "psychological noir." Cooper's intuitions and visions, the paranormal informative-

---

[9] Hague, "Infinite Games," 130, quoting Ronald Knox, "A Detective Story Decalogue," in *Detective Fiction: A Collection of Critical Essays*, ed. Robin W. Winks (Woodstock, CT: Foul Play Press, 1988), 200-201.

ness of his dreams, of his sleep-deprived and possibly hallucinatory states, might be chalked up to little more than coincidence in some cases, subliminal perception and unconscious reasoning in others—the latter two, common analogues of a well documented condition known as "blindsight."[10] At almost every turn, in fact, *Twin Peaks* provides its viewers with enough raw material for a naturalistic reading.

But a naturalistic reading of *Twin Peaks* runs up against pretty stiff competition from precisely those supernatural appearances it works hard to reconfigure by reducing them to symbols. Viewing *Twin Peaks* supernaturalistically is at least as defensible as, and certainly no less plausible than, a naturalistic reading. BOB seems to be a malevolent spirit capable of possessing different human hosts, one attracted especially to those who fear him, whose weakness and moral turpitude make them particularly suitable hosts. BOB also emanates from, and returns to, the Red Room/Black Lodge/White Lodge, a spiritual realm accessible to gifted and altered states of consciousness as well as—at the right time and place, and with the right emotional keys ("Fear and love open the door")—physically. On this tack, we cannot reduce Cooper's intuitive procedures, synchronistic insights, "Tibetan method," or invocation of magic to mere implicit reasoning, subtle perceptiveness, and luck. BOB is taken not as symbolic or fictional but as real, on this reading, no less real in the realm of *Twin Peaks* than Cooper himself or the RR's cherry pie. BOB is *reified* (from the Latin *re*, for thing), a real entity, a bona fide being. Such metaphysics and methods are naturally anathema to a naturalistic reading, and as such, anathema to noir.

Which is the better interpretation here, the naturalistic or the supernaturalistic? This is a difficult question. There is a legitimate sense in which, focusing on the viewer's aesthetic pleasure as the sole criterion, whichever (if either) interpretation better fosters a person's aesthetic experience of an artwork, that is the preferred, the better interpretation (for that person).[11] A naturalistic reading might work better for me, a supernaturalistic one for you, without contradiction. If, however, we have reason to want something more, some intersubjective standard, an interpretation that provides a best explanation of the data (details, elements) provided by the work, *Twin Peaks* leaves

---

[10]For more on this counterintuitive, philosophically provocative condition, see Jason Holt, *Blindsight and the Nature of Consciousness* (Peterborough, ON: Broadview, 2003).

[11]Jason Holt, "The Marginal Life of the Author," in *The Death and Resurrection of the Author?* ed. William Irwin (Westport, CT: Greenwood Press, 2002), 74-75.

us with a dilemma. To reduce or reify? That is the question. Notice how this interpretive dynamic is at work in the discussion that occurs immediately after resolution of the Laura Palmer case. Sheriff Truman opens with a comment on the recently deceased Leland:

TRUMAN: He was completely insane.

COOPER: Think so?

ALBERT: But people saw BOB. People saw him in visions—Laura, Maddy, Sarah Palmer.

MAJOR: Gentlemen, there's more in heaven and earth than is dreamt of in our philosophy.

COOPER: Amen.

TRUMAN: Well, I've lived in these old woods most of my life. I've seen some strange things, but this is *way* off the map. I'm having a hard time believing.

COOPER: Harry, is it any easier to believe a man would rape and murder his own daughter, any more comforting?

TRUMAN: No.

MAJOR: An evil that great in this beautiful world. Finally, does it matter what the cause?

COOPER: Yes, because it's our job to stop it.

ALBERT: Maybe that's all BOB is, the evil that men do. Maybe it doesn't matter what we call it.

TRUMAN: Maybe not. But if he was real, if he was here, and we had him trapped, and he got away, where's BOB now?[12]

---

[12] *Twin Peaks*, episode 17 (following Lavery, *Full of Secrets*, 233, listed as 16 in video releases, which do not include the pilot). Director: Tim Hunter; writers: Mark Frost, Harley Peyton, Robert Engels. Original airdate: Dec. 1, 1990. Notice that Albert, the noir patter specialist, takes a decidedly uncharacteristic stance on BOB at first, only later returning to a more hard-boiled point of view. Note also the Major's paraphrase of the famous line from *Hamlet* (I.v.166-67), Cooper's disturbing equation of epistemic justification with psychological comfort (which fuels the moral concerns mentioned later), and the unwitting irony of Truman's answer, "No." The right answer is clearly "Yes," because the naturalistic explanation is much more justified, hence easier to believe in that sense, and more comforting, too, for in a naturalistic framework, the evil, horrible as it is, dies with Leland, but in a supernaturalistic one, BOB is free to go on wreaking havoc, death, and suffering.

As viewers, we have a relative epistemic advantage in that we see more of what goes on in Twin Peaks than the characters do, or could. Owing to this, and particularly to what viewers discover in the final episode, we may be tempted to lean slightly toward a supernatural reading. But it ultimately remains unclear which reading is better, or whether either is, whether BOB, vis-à-vis the official list of things in the Twin Peaks universe, should be penciled in or crossed off. Perhaps, then, after all, the dichotomy is a false one. As Diane Stevenson writes:

> The strange case of the killing of Laura Palmer can be accounted for either by paternal psychopathology or by demonic possession. The universe of *Twin Peaks* alternates between the psychological and the phantasmal, the physical and the metaphysical, and the boundaries between these realms are blurred. Such confusion of realms, such transgression of limits, such hesitation between a natural and a supernatural frame of reference, characterize... *the genre of the fantastic.*[13] (emphasis mine)

It is not just that *Twin Peaks* can be read either way but that the truth, how it should be read, lies between the two readings. The best interpretation seems to rule out neither reading, yet falls short, on pain of clear contradiction, of wholly affirming both. Whether works of this kind constitute a definite genre, and whether this genre, if it is one, is aptly called "the fantastic" is a matter we may leave aside. The point is, aesthetically speaking, the dichotomy is a false one.

Open Interpretation

These considerations suggest an obvious question: Is it a good thing for an artwork to be interpretively open? We will now consider whether, and to what extent, the interpretive openness excluding *Twin Peaks* from the noir class is aesthetically desirable, and what, if so, this means for noir. So far we have engaged predominantly descriptive questions. It is time to address the evaluative side of the relationship.

Let us start by taking up some of the aesthetic and moral qualms we might have about interpretive openness. Generally, it might seem

---

[13]Diane Stevenson, "Family Romance, Family Violence, and the Fantastic in *Twin Peaks*," in Lavery, *Full of Secrets*, 70. Stevenson appeals to Tzvetan Todorov, *The Fantastic*, trans. Richard Howard (Ithaca, NY: Cornell University Press, 1975).

that we do a work, or ourselves, a disservice by failing to narrow down possible interpretations to a precise, closed, best one. But while this tack is plausible in connection with a scientific account of certain aspects of the world, the notion that artworks always—if ever—yield single, univocal interpretations, irrespective of permissibly variable purposes and standards, is easily countered.[14] Instead of such general misgivings about interpretive openness, we may have specific moral concerns about such interpretive openness as *Twin Peaks* exhibits. (Reread Cooper's disturbing line in the dialogue above, and see note 10.) Even if we do not reify BOB outright, keeping him in limbo between reduction and reification might seem to overshadow, diminish the significance of, aestheticize, and, worse, mitigate the horror of father-daughter abuse and murder.[15] From a consequentialist perspective, this might be a legitimate concern, although it is not clear how a BOB-inclusive aesthetic would transfer to our view of other works, much less make the leap—as BOB himself fictionally does—into the real world, tranquilizing or blinding us to such harsh truths. We know better. We know too much. It would seem more realistic, less evasive, to address the matter, and in a negative light, as *Twin Peaks* does, than to fail to broach it at all.

Some doubt might linger that interpretive openness of the sort in *Twin Peaks* is aesthetically desirable, and so it might be helpful to take another illustrative case. While there are many such across the arts, it seems best to use another breakthrough television series exhibiting strong interpretive openness and noirishness to boot. I have in mind *The Prisoner*, which has a number of crucial, yet interpretively open, elements. Throughout the series, it is unclear which side in the Cold War controls the Village, where Number 6 (Patrick McGoohan) is imprisoned. In the series finale, Number 6 finally meets Number 1, the mysterious, previously unseen agent in charge of his imprisonment, an apparently insane version of himself. This revelation invites us to read the series as a psychological allegory and yet falls short of establishing, as merely symbolic, the unreality of all the preceding events composing almost the entire series. Similarly, the finale's final shot, Number 6 in his sports car zipping down a sun-drenched highway, suggests a variety of possible interpretations: a loop back to the start of the series, a metaphor for freedom regained—or perhaps for freedom pos-

---

[14]Holt, "Marginal Life," 75-76.

[15]See Christy Desmet, "The Canonization of Laura Palmer," in Lavery, *Full of Secrets*, 93-108; and Diana Hume George, "Lynching Women: A Feminist Reading of *Twin Peaks*," in the same volume, 109-19.

sessed all along—optimistically that all psychosis leads to freedom, or pessimistically, given the loop, that freedom leads to psychosis. These elements force the interpretation here wide open, and the provocative aesthetic appeal of the series is clearly enhanced, not compromised, as a result. Such interpretive openness most strikingly distinguishes series like *The Prisoner* and *Twin Peaks* from those less aesthetically rewarding.

This might seem, by implication, to undermine the aesthetic quality of noir, casting it in a pale light, too pale a light, really, since such works as *The Maltese Falcon*, which would be corrupted by the kind of interpretive openness in *Twin Peaks*, are hardly of inferior grade. It could be that, aesthetically speaking, interpretive openness is simply desirable without being strictly necessary. Admittedly, *The Maltese Falcon* is not interpretively open in the same way, or to the same degree, as *Twin Peaks*. It is naturalistic, thoroughly so. But this does not mean that it is not, even significantly, interpretively open. The aesthetic appeal of *The Maltese Falcon* arguably depends on a kind of interpretive openness, psychological indeterminacy. Consider the prime example of the values that guide Sam Spade through the noir labyrinth. Beyond self-preservation via solving the mystery, there seems to be far more to Spade's motivation than we may initially suspect. Yet it is not clear whether he is moved by stoically silent compassion for his dead partner, a desire to avenge his partner's death, sexual desire for the prototype femme fatale, a cruel wish to punish her, wealth in the wake of finding the Falcon, an intrinsic desire to crack the case, the principled aim of trying to redress the injustices and have the wrongdoers held accountable, the practical aim of avoiding what would be bad for business, or preventing on a wider scale what would be "bad for every detective everywhere." All are plausible; none is clearly and decisively his. Spade's is a kind of existential project, to be sure, but his psychologically uncertain status remains, and remains piquant, even in his fainthearted attempts to explain himself (citing, in turn, the last three reasons in the list above). These may be convincing enough on their own, but they do not at all seem to strike Spade himself that way. Even if we accept Spade's explanations, however, it is not without legitimate doubt. Less aesthetically satisfying noirs leave much less open. Note the unnecessary, irksome expatiations on personal motives and poetic justice in *The Postman Always Rings Twice*. While interpretive openness is a good thing to have in art, the degree of appropriate openness is contextually variable.

For obvious reasons, the fantastic, like *Twin Peaks*, is more open than the realistic, noir included, which limits without eliminating openness per se.

The Omissive Aesthetic

As a last remark, it seems appropriate to highlight the connection between interpretive openness and what might be called the "omissive" aesthetic, the poignancy of *leaving out*, of letting some things remain unsaid, undepicted, unshown, which is quite possibly a characteristic of all artwork. Good artwork, moreover, seems to have it more than most. Leaving things out opens up interpretation. The less left unsaid, the more clumsy, telegraphed, artless the work. The other extreme, except in rare cases (some abstract and conceptual art), is likely equally insufficient for the purposes of art. Enough content and structure must be given to prompt, and delimit within manageable bounds, an audience's engagement. Having to read between the lines, bringing, as an appreciator, something *to* the work, and doing some work oneself, is an irreplaceable part of an ideal, perhaps of any *real*, artistic transaction. Work that allows enough space for this, that elicits rewarding intellectual contemplation in tandem with deep emotional response, is valuable as such, precisely for that reason. By leaving the metaphysics, hence the interpretation, open as it does, *Twin Peaks* exhibits the omissive in art and affords such aesthetic rewards.[16]

---

[16]I am most grateful to Steven M. Sanders and Aeon J. Skoble for invaluable comments and criticisms, from the initial framing of this paper to revising it for print, and to Marc Ramsay and Ami Harbin for enjoyable shared viewing and provocative discussion of *Twin Peaks*.

14   An Aesthete *par Excellence*

We see him from behind, his hair slicked back toward us, the simplicity of a white t-shirt that seems somehow elegant despite the setting. The left hand splays open a book of poetry for eyes that savor it at leisure. Not much later, the book lies on a table, in the same incongruous setting, with notes of piano in the air, Bach's "Goldberg Variations" coming from a tape recorder—the table a spread of drawings lovingly detailed from an eidetic memory and keen imagination by a surgically skilled hand. This is a pure aesthetic moment, yet also an overture, we know already, to a very different kind of scene.

This aesthetic moment belongs to Dr. Hannibal Lecter in *The Silence of the Lambs,* right before he butchers a pair of guards, cutting the face off one for an impromptu mask, stylizing the corpses in effecting his unlikely escape from the cell where the Memphis police have temporarily caged him. The soundtrack crescendos as Dr. Lecter, with a nightstick in tempo with the music, rains blow after blow on one of the guards—on us, in fact—seen from the guard's perspective in an inspired use of the subjective cam.

One may be tempted to interpret these scenes, the aesthetic moment and the butchery, as discontinuous, to think of the aesthetic moment as fake, a kind of camouflage used by Lecter to lull his captors into a false sense of only mild insecurity. Even the stylized guard's corpse strung up on the cage may seem but a diversion to draw attention from the literally face-masked Lecter posing supine as the other guard. But although these strategic benefits are undeniable, it makes more sense to interpret the scenes as continuous. Lecter's aesthetic appreciation is genuine, not disingenuous. The manner of stylization of the cage-pinned corpse clearly mattered to the one who posed it. Perhaps most importantly, it is apparently the same music, more fully orchestrated, that crescendos, a metronome for the nightstick blows, as if the nightstick is Lecter's gruesome conductor's baton. We also know from earlier that the butchery will have left Lecter's heartbeat unaccountably, inhumanly, chillingly calm and steady. Afterwards, the blood-spattered carnage everywhere, the piano reasserts itself as if under the light touch of Lecter's rhythmically gliding hand.

What gives this progression of scenes continuity is the simple fact that Hannibal Lecter, enigmatic monster that he is, is an *aesthete*, one who prizes the rewards, the pleasures, afforded by art and beauty: art, in its various styles, whatever it depicts—and whatever its raw materials; beauty, in its different forms, wherever it might be found, in however unlikely a place. For the aesthete, such pleasures don't just matter, they matter *a lot*, as they do for Lecter, who isn't just an aesthete but an aesthete *par excellence*. Such aestheticism is in fact the very key to unlocking the mystery of his character, elaborated as it is into such an alien, such a grotesque extreme that few if any could wish for the strength of stomach to follow.

This perspective makes an implicit assumption about the relative importance of various depictions of Dr. Lecter. Setting aside the seminal novels by Thomas Harris, I take Sir Anthony Hopkins's portrayal to be canonical, prominently though not exclusively in Jonathan Demme's 1991 masterpiece *The Silence of the Lambs*. This makes sense given the undisputed pop cultural preeminence of Hopkins's Lecter and Demme's *Silence*. Sir Anthony, alongside his significant body of film work, is notably also a composer and painter, a true artistic polymath; no wonder his portrayal of Lecter throws into sharp relief the doctor's aestheticism. That said, I'll always have a soft spot for Brian Cox's inaugural movie portrayal in *Manhunter*, which deemphasizes, at least by comparison, the doctor's aestheticism. The aesthetic is more evident in the Gaspard Ulliel effort in *Hannibal Rising*, its culinary and gastronomic side full-blown in *Hannibal*, both Hopkins's film and Mads Mikkelsen's TV incarnations.

Discriminating Taste

For aesthetes, art and beauty occupy a more prominent place in their value system than for most other people. Aesthetic value, the value of art and beauty, can be understood in contrast to other sorts of value, in particular intellectual and moral values. Consider as the ultimate trio of values the *good*, the *true*, and the *beautiful*, respectively the realms of moral, intellectual, and aesthetic value. Forget the problematic equations of the poet Keats (truth = beauty) and philosopher Plato (the good = the true = the beautiful), and appreciate that, in their ordinary senses, these terms are representative of entirely distinct values. In simple terms, being a good person has nothing to do with being smart or attractive, just as being smart has nothing to do with being attractive (which philosophers have lamented since Socrates) or good, just as possessing beauty has nothing to do with being a good or intelligent person. As an intellectual aesthete, Dr. Lecter clearly prizes two of these values very highly, leaving the other, we know which, an irrelevant castoff. A thing will have aesthetic value because of its power to provoke aesthetic experience, and for aesthetes such experiences are among life's greatest pleasures.

What makes an experience an *aesthetic* experience? It's a particular pleasure associated with the appreciation of art and beauty. Whether you're enjoying a painting of the sunset or the actual sunset, both enjoyments may count as aesthetic. You like looking at them, how you feel in, and reflect on, the moment of looking. Think of how you feel when you're listening to your favorite song, or watching a beloved movie. The pleasures, the thoughts and feelings that come in actively appreciating these works of art, that's what gives the experience an aesthetic quality. This is partly a kind of detachment. Think of Lecter's steady pulse when butchering his victims, or the way you respond to a nude study differently than to porn. At the same time, there's a kind of intensity of response in appreciating art, a keenness of attention, more focused and significant than in most ordinary experiences. What makes such "detached engagement" so rewarding, not just to aesthetes, is that it resolves internal conflicts, with intellectual and emotional responses in harmonious balance, in sharp contrast to everyday life.

Your aesthetic appreciation of art, or anything really, can be informed and enhanced in different ways. Lecter, for instance, has an extensive knowledge of art history, not to mention a medical doctor's appreciation of human anatomy, which, together with his fine drawing abilities, perhaps surprisingly recalls Leonardo da Vinci. Seriously, if you look at da Vinci's anatomical drawings, I challenge you not to see just a little bit of Lecter there! But the doctor also has other types of knowledge and know-how relevant to his aestheticism. These include a surgeon-grade precision with a scalpel, which mirrors the rendering precision of his sketch pencil, along with chef-worthy culinary chops—

where taste meets taste. Taste in either sense also depends on the taster's level of perceptual sophistication, on how well they discriminate the relevant properties of what they're judging: connoisseurship, in essence. Think of Lecter's olfactory prowess, and his particular penchant for an exotic sort of acquaintance with mundane humanity. Here looms a potential feedback loop: aesthetic pleasure motivates improving its underlying knowledge, skill, and discrimination, which in turn enhances further pleasure.

One thing that hasn't been mentioned yet but must be is the affinity between art and play. The psychopath's attitude toward their victims is often very much cat to mouse, or player to plaything. Play in its purer forms involves the freedom, responsiveness, and creativity of art, with a similar type of enjoyment. We know what fun Lecter has with anagrams and other wordplay, the half hints of coded puzzles—"If one does what God does enough times, one will become as God is" (Mann, *Manhunter*)—with reluctant playmates Graham and Starling, who are unwilling, unlike Lecter, to treat it as a game. In fact, Lecter doesn't exactly view Graham or Starling as mice so much as potential cats, as far as the game is concerned. He even handicaps himself, suggesting possible moves to *Manhunter*'s Graham: "You haven't threatened to take away my books yet"; to *Silence*'s Starling: "No, no, no, you were doing fine. You'd been courteous and receptive to courtesy, you had established trust with the embarrassing truth about Miggs, and now this ham-handed segue into your questionnaire? Tut-tut-tut, it won't do." This, of course, is just an entrée into what Lecter really wants to play: a game of quid pro quo.

Lecter's attitude toward serial killing, half playful, half serious, reflects his aestheticism, which cuts a very wide swath in being able to take aesthetic pleasure from things that most of us would find utterly repulsive. Many people prefer even their aesthetic encounters to be with rather lighter fare. Many moviegoers would opt for the lightness of a romantic comedy over the darkness of a Hannibal Lecter film. Such preferences are fine, of course, but art history is chock-full of aesthetically powerful works depicting not just dark but horrific things: Goya's disturbing painting of Saturn cannibalizing his son, for instance. As far as *depictions* go, of course, most of us understand aesthetic pleasure taken in a Goya painting or Demme film depicting cannibalism. We stop, however, at the divide between fiction and reality. *But Lecter doesn't stop.* He's able to derive aesthetic pleasure from, not just the depiction, but also the *reality* of such horror. Nor is it horror that matters to him, otherwise he wouldn't be so harsh a critic of other serial killers, or so technical in preparing a dish. Lecter is above all *discriminating*. He'd reject a Nazi aestheticism, cigarette cases and lampshades made from human skin, not as extreme evil—as we would—but as extreme bad taste. Such a hate-based aesthetic would strike him as utterly stupid. Lecter only really hates people who've been evil to him—or rude.

Blindness That Enhances

Being blind is something most people don't have much experience with, especially permanent blindness. We do, however, like Clarice Starling in Buffalo Bill's basement toward the end of *Silence*, have some sense of what it's like to have situational blindness, as nicely conveyed by Demme's use of the subjective cam giving us the killer's night-vision-goggled perspective on Starling's fumbling in the dark. Most of us think, however, and it is almost clichéd to say so, that blind people sometimes find that their condition has an upside, that the blindness is associated with, and the basis of, enhanced abilities in other areas. For instance, many blind people have improved spatial memory, and more sensitive nonvisual sensory perception: improved hearing, more sensitive touch. From a neuroscientific viewpoint, the explanation of this phenomenon is pretty straightforward, in that lacking visual input, some of the brain is essentially freed up and can contribute to other sorts of processing. Remember Reba McLean, Dollarhyde's coworker in *Manhunter*, running her fingers through the sedated tiger's fur, feeling its breath on her forearm, listening to its heartbeat?

Consider an analogy I would like to suggest between literal blindness and the metaphor of a psychopath being *morally* blind. A psychopath fails to see the moral dimensions of what they do and the moral status of other people, or they understand morality but fail to see the point of it. Lecter's psychopathy is blended with an intelligence too brilliant to be lacking an understanding of moral issues. Rather, his personal code of values and integrity aside, he just doesn't care. I'm thinking it's still appropriate to call this a kind of moral blindness, even though it's less a matter of not detecting the morally relevant features of a situation—for instance, that a potential victim is a *person*—and more a matter of ignoring these features, of being unmoved by them where the rest of us, in different degrees, would be so moved.

One of the fascinating aspects of Lecter's character is that it shines a spotlight on values and abilities that he has but that are not intermixed, unlike most of us, with muddying shades of morality: the evil genius, the amoral aesthete. The psychopath's moral deficit in this way shows such qualities as they do possess—in Dr. Lecter's case, a brilliant intelligence and sophisticated aesthetic sensibility—in starker, purer outline, in a way allowing us to appreciate these qualities and the beauty and significance of such abilities for what they are in themselves. For this reason Lecter is a kind of abstraction, from morality, of intelligence and aestheticism. Without the pure psychopathy we would have a more complicated, more realistic representation of a sophisticated and aesthetically sensitive intelligence. By being what he is, Lecter helps us appreciate just how important, and often unnoticed, the aesthetic is in our lives, from enjoying popular artworks like Hannibal Lecter films to savoring everyday rituals like your morning cup of coffee. With more or less sensuality, more or less aestheticism, we may relish eating a well-prepared liver—though we'd be pickier than Lecter, and less picky too, about what kind of liver.

Unlike Dr. Lecter, most of us are comparatively blind to the importance of the aesthetic in life. But of course, Lecter is blind to our moral concerns. Perhaps, as with a literal blindness that enhances other senses, it is precisely Lecter's moral blindness that enhances his powers of aesthetic discrimination, along perhaps with his astonishing olfactory sensitivity and gustatory breadth. We know he can identify perfumes and colognes on habitual wearers—Graham's Old Spice, Starling's L'Air du Temps—and this surely informs his sensitive palate. Smell, of course, is a primitive sense, an evolutionarily old, beastly sense, and this is retained, regardless of how sophisticated, how intellectualized it is, in Lecter's aesthetic sensibility. He seems more able to appreciate art than most of us, even those with some claim to the title aesthete. Just consider his stint as an art scholar in *Hannibal*. It may be—though let's hope not!—that having a Lecter-like aesthetic sophistication depends on a Lecter-like psyche.

The ACME Question

Part of what makes Hannibal Lecter a compelling, even archetypal, character is that we can't quite figure him out. He can figure out what makes *us* tick—those in his various peer groups: serial killers, psychiatrists, profilers—but we can't, it seems, figure out what makes *him* tick, whatever we learn of his formative years in *Hannibal Rising*. He's an enigma. Or as Will(iam Petersen's) Graham puts it *Manhunter*, when asked what was diagnosed as wrong with Lecter, "Psychologists call him a psychopath. They don't know what else to call him." But he's also, even among other psychopathic killers, a most unusual case, which we see with crystal clarity when we're introduced to him in *Silence*, last cell on the left. He's a completely different beast from the other criminally insane inmates: "They don't have a name for what he is." Nor is this just a matter of education, intelligence, or decorum. Lecter defies analysis. He's too smart, too unusual, for conventional understanding and techniques: "He's much too sophisticated for the standard tests" (Demme, *Silence*). As *Manhunter*'s Graham puts it, "We tried sodium amytal on him three years ago to find where he buried a Princeton student; he gave 'em a recipe for potato chip dip." As serial killers go, Lecter is clearly a cut above.

Now I'm not suggesting that we can necessarily fully plumb Dr. Lecter's psyche, not at all. Although we might, but perhaps never should, resolve the enigma he presents, it may prove insightful to seek at least a partial account of his character by considering what I'm calling here *the ACME question*. Specifically, if there is some hypothesis we can make about Lecter that can help explain different, seemingly incongruous, but essential aspects of his personality, that fact will give us good reason to accept that hypothesis: a curve that best fits a set of data points will be justified for that reason. This principle of "inference to the best explanation" is familiar both in philosophy and in science, and applies even in the case of fictional entities like Hannibal Lecter. The ACME question concerns and comprises four of these essential and ill-fitting aspects of Dr. Lecter's personality: 'A' for art, 'C' for cannibalism, 'M' for murder, 'E' for etiquette—each of which is vitally important to Lecter, though the set seems ill-matched. Why would someone who values brutal murder care about fine art? How could a cannibal's decorum give Emily Post a run for her money? Is there anything about Lecter that integrates and explains this apparently ragtag collection of tendencies?

Of course: the aesthetic. It's Lecter's aesthetic sensibility that underlies and unifies these different aspects of his concern and personality, at once ultra-civilized and ultra-savage. Lecter's appreciation for art isn't at all motivated by financial investment or cocktail-party snobbery. His art-scholar expertise rather expresses and facilitates his appreciation of works of art *as* works of art: for what they represent, what they express, for the skill and style with which they're created, and for the aesthetic pleasure that comes from interpreting and creating them. His cannibalism is no less refined. He's a gourmet, after all, a cannibal gourmet—both as a chef, where he exhibits a subtle creativity adapting Cordon Bleu techniques to preparing human tissue, and as an epicure, where he demonstrates an appreciative and discerning palate. Though he sometimes, in the form of attack, tears into live unprepared flesh with his teeth, this is not the aesthetic Lecter aspires to and often achieves. He prefers a slow burn. Lecter's attitude toward serial murder is similar, as he's quite at home adopting the posture of both artist and critic. As an artist he creates difficult, often symbolically rich tableaux using his victims as raw material. As a critic he often demeans the imperfect efforts—as psychologically shallow, forensically clumsy, interpretively trite—of other serial killers.

But how does Dr. Lecter's odd obsession with etiquette fit in here? His first murder, we see in *Hannibal Rising*, is spurred by the victim's bad behavior toward Lecter's aunt: menacing but essentially disrespectful. In *Silence*, after his escape, Starling is convinced that Lecter won't come after her because "he would consider that rude." In general—that is, when he's not killing or eating anyone—except for occasional bouts of provocative rudeness, he's scrupulously polite and decorous. Those like Graham and Starling who respect him, in both senses, likewise refer to him, title intact, as "*Dr.* Lecter." To them, and up to a point, Lecter responds in kind. If we think of etiquette as a set of arbitrary conventions which are essential to culture, part of the order that civilization imposes on nature, then we can see how someone like Lecter who's fastidious about etiquette may be that way because in a world of chaos such politesse can provide deep aesthetic satisfaction. "Discourtesy," says Lecter, "is unspeakably ugly to me"— an aesthetic complaint (Demme, *Silence*).

In short, although this doesn't and isn't meant to dispel completely the enigma that is Dr. Hannibal Lecter, what unifies his value system, what integrates his personality, what makes him the archetype he is, is precisely the aesthetic. Yet what makes sense of Lecter makes sense of us, the audience, as well, and what we—through the horror—keep coming back for.

Permissions

Index

Dickie, G., 8, 80-1
Dickinson, E., 107
diencephalon, 18, 21, 62
Dionysus, 22, 61, 86
discrimination, 109, 180, 182
Djinn (Robbe-Grillet), 29
D.O.A. (Maté), 154, 156
D.O.A. (Morton and Jankel), 154-6
DOA, *see* death of the author thesis
Don Quixote (Cervantes), 42
Dostoevsky, F., 35, 37
Double Indemnity (Wilder), 162, 167
downbeat ending, 147, 152-3, 156, 160-1
Doyle, A.C., 170
dream, 22, 29, 165, 170-2
driftwood art, 60
Duchamp, M., 14, 63-6, 81, 87
Dylan and Cohen, 95
Dylan, B., 95-7

écriture thesis, 33
Eliot, T.S., 35, 46
emotion, 10, 17-8, 21-3, 40, 61-2, 71-7, 85, 87, 104, 108-13, 116-28; real *vs.* make-believe, 120, 125-8; lower *vs.* higher, 122-6, 128
emotional response, 22, 40, 61, 73, 104, 111-2, 117-21, 124, 176, 179
entertainment, 103, 109, 119
equipoise, 61, 85
essentialism, 62, 64, 69
etiquette, 183-4
evolution, 61, 77, 85, 88, 122, 182

existential, 49, 97, 103, 141, 143, 146, 167, 175; atmosphere, 97, 146, 163, 167; commitment, 124, 127
expression, 10-12, 19-25; as graded, 10-11; objectified, 20, 23-5
expressionism, 71, 146, 148, 153, 170; abstract, 71; German, 146, 170
expressivism, 10, 12, 72

F-minor Concerto (Bach), 21
"Fabrizio's: Criticism and Response" (Allen), 105
fact/value distinction, 68, 161-2
Family Plot (Hitchcock), 134, 136
Famous Blue Raincoat (Warnes), 97
fandom, 93-5, 98
fantastic, 173, 176
fear, 17, 21, 115, 117-29, 169, 171
Fellini, F., 106
femme fatale, 150-2, 165-6, 175
fiction, 5, 28-30, 33, 36, 49, 54, 74, 115-29, 134, 138-9, 143, 146, 167, 170-1, 174, 180, 183
fictionalia, 121
film, 48, 96, 103-4, 106, 109-10, 115, 169-70, 178, 180, 182
film noir, 145-8, 152, 161-6, 168, 170
Fitzgerald, F.S., 108
Flaubert, G., 3, 110
fMRI, 87
formalism, 72
Foucault, M., 27-35, 41-3

191

193

195

About the author

Jason Holt is Professor in the School of Kinesiology at Acadia University, where he teaches courses in philosophy and communication. Previously he taught philosophy at the University of Manitoba, Concordia University, and Dalhousie University, after earning degrees from Acadia University (B.A. Honours), Dalhousie University (M.A.), and the University of Western Ontario (Ph.D.), all in philosophy. His research interests are varied, including aesthetics, philosophy and popular culture, philosophy of mind, and philosophy of sport. His books include *Blindsight and the Nature of Consciousness*, which was shortlisted for the Canadian Philosophical Association Book Prize, coauthored and edited volumes, and literary works, most recently a book of poetry, *Inversed*. He lives in Wolfville, Nova Scotia, Canada with his wife Megan.

www.ingramcontent.com/pod-product-compliance
Lightning Source LLC
Chambersburg PA
CBHW052040090426
42739CB00010B/1990